The
unGuide to Dating

The unGuide to Dating

A HE SAID/SHE SAID ON RELATIONSHIPS

Camerin Courtney
and Todd Hertz

Revell
Grand Rapids, Michigan

Published by Fleming H. Revell
a division of Baker Publishing Group
P.O. Box 6287, Grand Rapids, MI 49516-6287

Printed in the United States of America

Library of Congress Cataloging-in-Publication Data
Courtney, Camerin, 1971–
    The unguide to dating : a he said/she said on relationships / Camerin
Courtney and Todd Hertz.
        p.   cm.
    Includes bibliographical references.
    ISBN 0-8007-3076-3 (pbk.)
    1. Dating (Social customs) 2. Dating (Social customs)—Religious
aspects—Christianity. 3. Man-woman relationships. 4. Man-woman
relationships—Religious aspects—Christianity. I. Hertz, Todd, 1977–
II. Title.
HQ801.C733 2005
241'.6765—dc22   2005021796

Portions of this book were previously published on www.ChristianSinglesToday .com and in *Today's Christian Woman* magazine, ministries of Christianity Today International.

Out of respect for our friends and exes, many names and details have been changed throughout this book.

Contents

Introduction   7

1. State of the Date: A Strange New World   13
2. The Dating Drought: Why Aren't Christian Singles Dating?   31
3. Men in the Church: O Brother, Where Art Thou?   43
4. Changing Gender Roles: You've Come a Long Way, Baby?   55
5. Making the First Move: Still Only a Man's Job?   69
6. Dating Non-Christians: The Appeal of the Forbidden Fruit   87
7. Internet Dating: Using a Mouse to Find a Spouse?   97
8. Matchmaking: Something Old, Something New, Someone Borrowed, Someone Blue   107
9. TV Dating: Reality Bites   119
10. Sexual Temptation: True Love Waits . . . for What?   131
11. Body Image: The Good, the Bad, and Those Who Feel Ugly   147
12. Biological Clock: The Parent Trap   163

Contents

13. Intergender Friendships: Risks, Rewards, and Recreational
    Kissing—Is It Really That Weird?   173
14. Breaking Up: The Remains of the Date   187

    Acknowledgments   203
    Notes   205

Introduction

Camerin: I was watching an episode of one of those WB teen dramas recently when I got a feeling similar to the one I get when flipping through typical Christian dating books.

In the episode, two of the show's main characters were considering sleeping with their significant others, a first for both of these sixteen-year-olds. They deliberated; I cringed. They faced obstacles; I rejoiced. One of them gave in; my heart sank. But perhaps what bothered me most was the conversation the female of the two characters had with a close friend. Sprawled in one of their bedrooms, they discussed the pros and cons of the decision to "go all the way."

"Just don't wait too long," the friend advised. "You don't want to end up like Morgan, who's now twenty-nine and is so afraid she'll die a virgin." I let out a noise signaling my half amusement and half heartbreak. But mostly I sat curled up on my couch, feeling altogether silly to be "still dating" at twice these characters' age.

As I said earlier, I get a similar feeling when I browse the singles section at my local Christian bookstore. Nearly all of the books in this genre with a dating focus make me feel old and invisible and silly in their teen-centeredness. As with that TV show, the focus is on people half my age. But unlike them, I don't have classmates and a curfew. I don't have a youth group. Nor do I have a youth pastor's and my parents' watchful eyes keeping me accountable. I don't have proms and pimples (well . . .) and peer pressure.

What I do still have are hormones, first dates, crushes, temptations to date non-Christians, a sex-saturated society, a pop culture that preaches the religion of romance, good-night kisses (when I'm lucky!), breakups (when the luck runs out), exes, and dry spells.

But as a thirty-four-year-old dater, I also have a solo apartment, a changing body, marriage on my mind, a biological clock that keeps tick-tick-ticking, family and church pressures to pair off, friends who are getting married and friends who are getting divorced, shifting demographics, and, consequently, an overall changing climate in which to date.

Unfortunately, no one's addressing these things. Dating advice within the church seems to peter out at around age eighteen. But with 40 percent of the adult population in the U.S. currently single, dating obviously continues past that age. And in a current cultural climate marked by *Desperate Housewives*, speed dating, and staggering divorce rates (oh my!), simple 1-2-3 formulas just don't cut it anymore. The dating world has gotten wacky and weird and altogether complex, and singleness discussions and advice need to reflect this reality if we're to take them at all seriously.

We Christian singles past the age of eighteen crave intelligent, credible voices to speak into this void and this mass confusion. At least, that's been one of the biggest lessons I've learned during my stint as a singles columnist for ChristianSinglesToday.com for the past five years. The best part of this gig, hands down, has been the reader feedback. While I love this peek into the minds and lives of my comrades in singlehood, it's staggering how many of these singles are surprised that others have similar experiences and feelings. Whenever I share a dating (or lack thereof) frustration, observation, joy, conundrum, or temptation, I receive countless emails from single readers exclaiming, "You too? I'm so glad to know I'm not the only one who has this experience/feels this way/is this neurotic!" I've learned that a little bit of vulnerability leads to a lot of conversation. And a lot of conversation leads to better understanding in the face of all the confusion about the strange new world of dating.

This dynamic of conversation leading to better understanding certainly proves true whenever I talk to my co-worker friend Todd. Whenever he pops into my office for some dating advice or sympathy or bragging, or IMs me about his utter bewilderment with the female of the species, or calls me to rant and rave about the latest dating-oriented reality TV show, we have great eye-opening discussions. I've explained many a female eccentricity (yes, we know we're emotional, and no, we can't have enough shoes), and it's been so enlightening to get a peek into the male mind. Similar to what I've found with my singles columns, great things have come from our willingness to be honest, dig deep, share our unique gender perspectives, avoid pat answers, and live with the messiness that's just part of the territory on this journey of dating, and singlehood, and life in general.

It was in all those conversations and in all those emails that the idea for this book was born—to extend to even more singles the benefit of vulnerability, peer voices, a recognition of daters of all ages, formula-less insights, some clarity and comfort, discussion of new pop-culture trends, and acknowledgment of how tricky it's gotten to find love in a postmodern age.

TODD: I'm sick of trying to wear the right shoes. You see, it's one of those things we single guys are told: women pay attention to shoes. *With fancy shoes*, I think, *I might find the right girl*. The problem I've found with this theory is that the people telling us to wear the right shoes to impress women . . . are women. Guys, or at least *this* guy, have no clue what the "right shoes" are.

And I'm betting that since those fancy shoes are meant to impress the gender that wears open toes and eight-inch heels, these shoes probably aren't very practical for playing touch football or feeding cattle. (Of course, I don't feed cattle. But if I suddenly had to, I wouldn't want to be stuck doing it in those fancy shoes.)

For a while, I began thinking that my lack of the right shoes, the right pants, or the right kitchen abilities was why I wasn't finding "the one." I was in my midtwenties and alone. *Something must be wrong*, I thought. So I started reading up on what I was supposed to do to find a mate. Be seen being nice to babies. Bake stuff. Buy candles and wine. Open doors and smell nice. But no matter what I did, I got no closer to marriage.

Of course, there's nothing wrong with self-improvement—taking care of yourself, being a gentleman, and becoming a more well-rounded individual. I definitely want to keep learning who I am and making myself the best person I can be—regardless of whether there's a spouse in my future. The problem is the *reason* I was making some of these changes.

All too often we read books or hear advice that say there are formulas for finding happiness, methods to attracting a spouse. Dating books promise "steps to finding the perfect mate." Friends and family, while not asked, imply we must be doing something wrong if we're still single. And too easily we think it must be because we aren't attractive enough.

But none of this is true. Despite what many Christian dating books suggest, there's no formula for love. There's no one thing we can do better and—*poof!*—we're married. Besides, this journey isn't just about us—we're also trying to follow God's will. And nope, there are no hard-and-fast rules on how God will work. But I know this: we cannot predict how he will work, and we shouldn't try to limit his ways by saying they follow rules or steps. Some people meet their spouse in high school. Some meet on the Internet, or by speed dating, or even while feeding cattle. We cannot predict the methods God will use.

True, there are things in our lives all of us can work on. Maybe we can better "circulate" ourselves by getting out there and trying to meet more people. Maybe we can choose to look for ways to make our lives more fulfilling or improve ourselves. And of course, we can work to better our relationship with Christ and grow to better discern God's will for our singleness and lives. Over the last couple of years, I've fought to lose weight and improve my patience. I'd like to think I've learned to dress a little better. And, living alone, I've had to figure out how to cook. Sure, these are all preparing me to be a better spouse if that's in God's plan. But they aren't merit badges to pin on my sash until I eventually earn a wife. And they're not cures to a "singleness" illness. They're just ways I'm stretching myself one art class here and Bible study there.

It's not always easy to remember this lesson, though. Every year I get farther away from the age at which my parents got married makes me wonder, *Am I doing something wrong?* And like Camerin said, it's hard to find voices in the Christian media who understand what singleness is like on the other side of twenty-five and who aren't making us feel as though the problem must be something we're doing wrong (like not wearing fancy, impractical shoes).

That's why Camerin and I wanted to share our insights, thoughts, and bewilderments—and those of friends, acquaintances, and even random strangers—as we navigate all the pressures, trends, and temptations in this strange new world of dating for grown-ups. We don't have all the answers. But we're two singles who'd like to share this journey with you in this *unGuide to Dating*.

I

State of the Date

A Strange New World

Camerin: Here's how it used to be: Boy meets girl. Boy asks girl on a date. Girl says yes, and they date happily ever after.

Here's how it more commonly is now: Girl realizes she isn't getting any younger and that the dating prospects at her church are slim. She's asked by the 212th well-wisher when she'll finally decide to get married. Girl signs up for online dating service. Girl peruses hundreds of personal ads, and emails many men. A year and many techno-dates later, she gives up and wonders if she should try speed dating—or join a convent!

Let's face it—dating has gotten complicated. With the advent of many new technologies, trends, pop-culture influences, and demographic dynamics, the traditional route to the altar has become as outdated as an Atari game system. But nearly all of us singles still want to find love and get married. So how do we get from here to there? Good question!

Before Todd and I take a stab at answers, we want to unpack a few of the dynamics that make up this strange new world. By looking at how we got to "here"—single and in an utter state of confusion—we're hoping we'll be better able to get to "there"—better equipped to navigate this strange new world of dating and to eventually end up happily hitched (if that's in God's plan).

From our experiences and observations, Todd and I have found that confusion stems from six key areas.

I KISSED JOSH HARRIS GOOD-BYE

TODD: I received a bizarre response from a Christian woman I asked out shortly after I graduated college. She was puzzled by the invitation and replied, "I'm sorry, I don't get asked out. I don't know what that means. I think we could go to a movie or something, but I don't understand what a date *means*."

Perhaps the key confusion in the Christian dating world is that no one really knows what "dating" is. What's a date? What kind of commitment does dating involve? Should we even be dating? Should we be courting instead? Should we just let our parents prearrange the whole thing and exchange some goats between families?

One reason for this confusion is simply that, like the girl I asked out, the majority of Christian singles just aren't dating much. (We'll explore this further in chapter 2.) If a Christian hasn't been asked out in three years, or is thirty and has never been in a relationship that's lasted longer than three months, there can be a great deal of confusion about dating.

While the Bible is our guidebook to living, it's largely silent about the meeting and getting-to-know-you process of romantic relationships. As Rob Marus, a singles minister who reviewed dating books in *Christianity Today* magazine, wrote, "If I were relying strictly on Scripture . . . I would be waiting for God to create a wife for me out of my rib."[1] Because of the lack of clear direction about dating in the Bible, we turn to what's being said in our Christian culture. This leads to the biggest contributor of confusion over what dating is: the mixed messages and divergent camps within Christianity.

Most Christians point to author Joshua Harris as the starter of the debate. "Josh Harris hasn't made my life any easier," Marus stated in his book review. "Thanks to him, my future wife . . . may very well have given up the idea of ever dating."[2]

In his 1997 book *I Kissed Dating Goodbye*, Harris wrote that dating isn't wrong, but like fast food, it's not the best option. His solution was a form of courtship (though he didn't use the word) he called "smart love." Basically, he defines it as developing a purposeful, accountable, and committed relationship based on sincere, God-focused love. He emphasized being motivated by a concern for others and not selfish desires. A flurry of books followed with ideas on how Christians should (or shouldn't) date.

"Christian singles are completely baffled by dating," wrote Benjamin, a reader of ChristianSinglesToday.com. "Many would agree there are some crazy ideas floating around evangelicalism today about the topic. By the time I graduated high school, the idea of dating had become so intimidating I almost gave up on the idea. There's no manual for dating or relationships, and neither kissing dating good-bye nor sitting at home is an adequate solution."

It's a confusing scene to figure out, and the confusion only grows when you're interested in someone. You have no idea what camp she's in. Has she kissed dating good-bye? Does she understand we're on a date? Do I owe her family any goats? Maybe we all should wear signs.

A typical story I hear over and over goes like this: Boy meets girl. They hang out, and boy behaves in the typical "courting" style for a couple months. They grow close. After a time, one asks for a vocal commitment, and the other replies, "Ummm, we're just friends."

It's confusing that so many different ideas exist within Christianity, but as Marus noted in *Christianity Today*, when you look closely, you may discover the problem is simply semantics. Jeramy Clark's *I Gave Dating a Chance* is a popular response to Harris's book. However, Harris and Clark basically use different words for the same thing—healthy, God-honoring relationships conducted with integrity. And come to think of it, maybe the fact that these notions are so similar is a good thing. If Christians focus on the concept of healthy, purposeful, God-honoring dating instead of wordplay, maybe some confusion over dating and courtship would diffuse.

But I still think signs would be helpful.

GIRL **POWER!**

 Camerin: I was watching *Kim Possible*, a popular Saturday morning cartoon, on a recent lazy weekend morning when I realized what a microcosm this show is for women's changing roles in society over the past several decades (who knew?). Kim is a high school cheerleader who saves the planet during her passing periods with the "help" of her bumbling-but-lovable male sidekick, Ron Stoppable. In stark contrast, when I was a kid, *Scooby Doo*, *Speed Racer*, and *Underdog* numbered among my animated favorites. These shows all had male protagonists, usually the show's namesake; the female characters—with telling names such as Polly Purebred and Danger-Prone Daphne—were mainly there to admire the male characters and provide comic relief. My, how times have changed! Now there's Kim and her fellow fictional chicks Eliza Thornberry, Lizzy McGuire, and those Powerpuff Girls. These girls have confidence, special powers, equality—if not superiority—to their male counterparts, and a world that

16

revolves around their latest crisis or accomplishment. Just ask any of these animated wonder kids—girl power is widespread, and here to stay!

As one who's always been more workaholic than domestic diva, I've been thrilled to watch women's roles expand and permeate our culture. I love that there are now female CEOs, professional athletes, politicians, and news anchors. I marvel that just a generation ago, my mom's main two options in college were nursing and education. Today, for the most part, the sky's the limit for us women. Universities are now turning out more female than male graduates . . . in every field of study imaginable. The National Center for Education statistics project that by 2010 there will be fifty-nine female grads for every forty-one male grads. Simultaneously, motherhood is becoming more respected for the remarkable job that it is—shaping individual lives and our collective future. Though there are still strides to make, pockets of gender prejudice, and vexing questions about women's role in the church, in many arenas women are being celebrated and liberated.

But with all this advancement and equality comes a whole heap of confusion relating to the opposite gender. As we've renegotiated our relationship with society, we've had to do the same with the gender that's had to bend and flex to our changing roles. As Polly Purebred has become Kim Possible, Speed Racer has become bumbling Ron Stoppable. As a result of all this renegotiation, I'm regularly flummoxed by small incidents throughout my day.

For example, when I approach a door with a male friend or co-worker, do I open it or allow him to do so? Part of me still loves it when a man displays a traditional act of chivalry, and yet part of me recognizes the utter logic of opening the door myself if I get there first. I mean, I do have arms! Similarly, when I'm out for lunch or coffee with a date, do I expect him to pay out of tradition? Do I offer to pay for us both, since I earn a salary too? Do we go dutch? What's the subtle implication of each option, and are these things really what I want to communicate? Among the biggest of all gender-confusion issues is whether or not it's OK for a woman to ask a man out on a date. Is this a healthy way for females to go after what we want, or is this an off-putting, too-aggressive move? I was surprised by the numerous impassioned, conflicting responses to this question when I posed it to readers of ChristianSinglesToday.com (more on that in chapter 5).

All of these questions come before a relationship is even established. Once a couple has navigated all this tricky terrain to establish some level of commitment to one another, there's a whole host of new questions to tackle about gender roles within the relationship. From a female's perspective, it can be tricky to find someone who not only shares your beliefs and has some common interests and mutual attraction, but also who shares a similar view on the role the woman should play in the home if the relationship leads to marriage (which is the ultimate issue at hand, no?). Are there similar views about whether or not you'll stay home with the children, once you have them? What about the popular option of homeschooling? In our current age, what does it look like for a man to be the head of the household, as is established in the Bible?

I hate to admit it, but with all this confusion, I sometimes secretly long for the simplicity of a time when all that was expected of me was an occasional flirty hair flip, adoring look, well-cooked meal, or well-behaved offspring. Going from damsel in distress to savior of the world is wonderfully liberating, empowering, and affirming—and yet simultaneously tiring, complicated, and unforeseen-repercussion laden. Not the least of these repercussions is the utter confusion we now have when even contemplating romantic relationships (more on this in chapters 4 and 5).

HERE'S THE CHURCH, HERE'S THE STEEPLE, WHAT ABOUT THE SINGLE PEOPLE?

TODD: Scene—Camerin's office:

- *Camerin:* So this guy is trying to fix you up with a girl who wants to be a missionary?
- **TODD:** Right. In a third-world country.
- *Camerin:* And you don't want to be a missionary?
- **TODD:** I'm uncomfortable at county fairs. Can you imagine me in Bolivia?
- *Camerin:* OK, so the missionary thing is an obstacle.
- **TODD:** And probably a sign that this isn't God's plan, right?
- *Camerin:* Well, you wouldn't want to rob a third-world country of a missionary, would you? I mean, I know you want a wife, but those folks probably want some food and medical help and the Truth.
- **TODD:** I guess it would be a tad selfish to say, "Sorry, Bolivia, this one's mine!"

There are boatloads of challenges unique to Christian singleness. On top of regular dating pressures, we also have to think about acting within God's will, about purity and integrity, and about living out our own calling to God's service. What if she's called to be a small-town Iowa pastor and me a doctor in Madagascar?

On top of that, I have myriad questions that confuse the issue when I meet a prospective date. How do I know if the cute girl in the grocery store is a Christian? Should I date someone in my Bible study or my church given the possible messiness if we break up? How do we reconcile differing beliefs within a shared faith? On top of all this mounting confusion, we add the fact that we aren't

19

just looking for a good time but are hoping to find "the one." Before we know it, we're not just talking about someone to get coffee with but considering if this person we've spoken to twice could be a good spouse and parent. It's as if I should be handing out twelve-page applications and requiring dental exams.

Well, it gets messier. As we're dating and trying to figure how God wants to use us in our singleness, we live in an evangelical Christian culture heavily steeped in the institution of marriage. Here's a message delivered to singles at Joshua Harris's New Attitude Conference in 2004. The speaker was Dr. Al Mohler, president of the Southern Baptist Theological Seminary. He said:

> I'm going to speak of the sin that I think besets this generation. It is the sin of delaying marriage as a lifestyle option among those who intend someday to get married, but they just haven't yet. . . . In heaven, is the crucible of our saint-making going to have been through our jobs? I don't think so. The Scripture makes clear that it will be done largely through our marriages. The longer you wait to get married, the more habits and lifestyle patterns you will have that will be difficult to handle in marriage. . . . If you're seventeen, eighteen, nineteen, twenty, or in your early twenties—what are you waiting for?

I don't agree that Christian singles are largely delaying marriage. I don't think marriage is the only place God uses us. And I don't think the majority of Christian singles view singleness as a lifestyle "option." But Dr. Mohler was right about one thing: some Christian singles are waiting to get married. I know I am. But I'm not delaying it, as he went on to say, so that I can put my career first or so I can sow my oats (I don't know if I even have oats!). Instead, I'm waiting for when I feel God is leading me to marriage. And I really *am* looking. I trust his purposes. Of course, figuring out his purposes isn't always easy. Another dating conundrum Christians face is figuring out that tricky line between trusting him and also doing our part. It's an easy out for us to be passive and just sit in our houses and wait for God to drop a spouse on our doorstep. (We'll talk more about this in chapter 4.)

Yes, Dr. Mohler is right: the Bible does regard marriage as a sacred institution. And I want to be a part of it. But is it really a sin to be single past twenty? What about Paul? What about Jesus? I believe God works in individual lives differently. What is good for one person isn't necessarily the right path for the next. And I honestly believe most Christian singles aren't purposely ignoring God's call to marry. We want marriage, but not with just *anyone*. We want a God-chosen spouse.

I don't think marriage is a cure-all that will make us more spiritually or sexually healthy or automatically better at serving in ministry. Some people in the church seem to regard marriage as a first-aid kit that makes everything better, so you'd better hurry up and get hitched.

For instance, I used to be involved in a weekly prayer meeting with a large group of Christians who were varied in background, denomination, and age. It was a blessing, but it had one sticky point. Only two of us were single. I asked for prayers one day about a relationship I was in. I knew the relationship was no longer leading to marriage, and I was preparing to end it. I said, "Things aren't good, and I could use prayers for guidance, because we now want very different things." One married man, in all seriousness, turned to me and said, "Why don't you just propose?"

Maybe it's because I'm part of the first real generation of divorce and have seen that Christians are in no way immune to divorce, but it scares me to think others are suggesting that singles just jump into marriage at a young age and assume everything will work itself out. Yes, God is healing. And he loves marriage, but we also have to feel God's blessing on our individual situations. Because it's hard to understand someone else's individual calling, many marrieds in the church just don't get us. And that leads to a lot of feelings of misunderstanding, bitterness, and loneliness. In my prayer group, I remember several prayers along the lines of "Lord, thank you for the beautiful gift of marriage and please hold these couples and relationships in your hands as they serve you." A lovely prayer for them; a left-out feeling for me.

"In my church, the singles in their twenties and thirties are gone—they're missing," says Angela, a reader of ChristianSinglesToday. com.

> It gets so lonely. Singles get discouraged when they attend church and there's such an emphasis on marriage. Churches don't seem to know what to do with singles. And so we don't find our place to serve, our role to play in our community of faith, and much-needed acceptance. Eventually, a lot of singles get discouraged and leave the church altogether. It's very sad, because where do they go? Yet another church?

If churches don't know what to do with singles, then it makes sense that they definitely don't know what to do with dating. A lot of Christians tend to marry young—during or immediately following college—and never really experience dating as adults. This leads to a lot of marrieds in our congregations who can't relate to us and our dating issues. And so the problem becomes that not only are singles largely absent on Sunday morning but also that no one is speaking to those of us there about what we're going through.

Not all hope is lost. While the confusion seems to be created by attitudes in the church at large, the solutions are in individuals.

When I broke up with the girl I asked for prayer about, a respected older married man gave me the support and advice that really comforted me. And when my head is swirling with questions, I have friends—single and married—who offer advice or just listen to me prattle on like Rain Man.

BRIDGET JONES AND BACHELOR BOB

Camerin: If messages from the church about dating seem mixed, or completely absent, those from our popular culture are certainly clear. In your face, you might say. And, for Christians, a tad troubling. While I loved it when TV shows such as *Friends*, *Ally McBeal*, and *Sex and the City* began to acknowledge my demographic, as well as all the countless quirks and neuroses that can accompany the single existence, I felt an undeniable disconnect between the messages of my culture and the realities of my faith. In between all the depictions of roommate issues, families of friends, dating disasters, and liberating solo moments, were common threads that don't jibe with my Christian beliefs: casual sex, living with a significant other, rampant materialism. This new brand of singles-centered entertainment established many assumptions about our demographic—namely that we're flitting from relationship to relationship, enjoying copious amounts of "liberating" casual sex in search of the ultimate salvation: Mr. or Ms. Right (or at least Mr. or Ms. Right Now).

These assumptions are backed up by countless other pop-culture entities: *The Rules*, *The Bachelor/The Bachelorette*, *Bridget Jones* and the entire brand of chick lit she launched, and romantic comedies such as *How to Lose a Guy in 10 Days*. Even Barbie ditched boring ol' Ken in a 2004 publicity stunt/act of single-girl liberation—there are so many other boy toys to check out! I've often joked with my single friends that I don't want to be single, I want to be single in a TV show or movie. I'd have a fabulous apartment in a big city, despite a solo income and a high cost of living; great designer duds, which I'd wear even while bumming around my abode; an amazingly fit body, even though there's hardly any time to work out; a tight-knit circle of like-minded, equally fascinating friends; and more romantic possibilities than I'd know what to do with.

But reality is much less scintillating (and much more mismatched). My Friday nights are usually spent at home alone with a takeout dinner and a rental flick (which, dare I admit, I usually find quite enjoyable). My apartment is small, my hips are wide. My only designer duds are the ones I bought on the cheap at TJ Maxx. Just when I establish a tight-knit family of friends, one of them moves or gets married or becomes a mom. And more often than not, I can count the time between dates in months and years—a trend that's sweeping Christian singledom (more on this in chapter 2). Of course, there's also the issue of morals—I actually have some. Even when I have dates and they turn out to be great, we aren't hopping in the sack or living together or making babies together even though we're "just friends" (a la Ross and Rachel).

This gulf between the pop-culture version of singleness and the Christian reality of singleness creates one big problem: the freak factor. The more we see and experience this dichotomy, the more we feel like big ol' freaks for obviously doing this whole singleness thing wrong. We can start to feel like we're the only singles spending Friday night alone, wearing mismatched sweats when we're hanging at home, experiencing searingly lonely moments, and just hoping for a date sometime this year, this decade, this lifetime. The hot-tub rendezvous or fly-to-Aruba version of dating on reality TV shows can make our simple coffee shop get-togethers seem altogether boring. And when we watch teenage characters on shows such as *The O.C.* or *One Tree Hill* having more sex than Heidi Fleiss, we start to feel like silly fuddy-duddies. And after a while, we become hesitant to share our real singleness experiences with even our Christian friends, withdrawing into ourselves for fear that others will look at us like we have three heads for finding Me Nights exceedingly enjoyable and for longing for a date, let alone a good-night kiss.

So, in the end, our pop-culture depictions of singleness lead to lots of assumptions about the single life. These assumptions lead to a huge disconnect for us single Christians. And this disconnect leads to potential isolation—and mostly all manner of confusion about what dating is, what dating looks like, how often it's happening, and what happens at the end of said dates.

FAMILY MATTERS (AND THEY DO MATTER, WHETHER WE LIKE IT OR NOT . . .)

TODD: Even death cannot stop my family's relentless onslaught upon my singleness.

Last year, I got the somewhat expected call one Saturday morning that my dad's father had died. Because I had half of my friend Jen's possessions in the back of my pickup truck (I was helping her move—not stealing), I couldn't go home right away. So, by the time I did arrive home, my family had already done all the initial preparations and meetings with the funeral home. Unfortunately, some family members already had some other plans in the works as well: to set me up with Stephanie, the funeral home coordinator. That's right, the woman planning my grandpa's burial.

The real trouble came when word spread about this "prospect." At the wake, a family member asked in all seriousness—*and* in front of family, our pastor, and some funeral home employees—"So, how're things going with Stephanie?"

Sure, my family means well. Yes, they love me for who I am and are intensely proud of who I am. But there's also an assumption from some of them that I'm not "well" enough until I get married. And apparently they think I need help getting to the altar.

Constant setup offers and questions such as "So, are you just not ready for marriage?" and "When are you going to decide to get married?" hurt. Even if we're sincerely happy with who we are and have resolved to make use of the single stage God has us in right now, these questions confuse us. We feel pulled in opposite directions. We doubt God's plan. *If my own family is making such a big deal about my singleness, maybe there is something wrong with me,* I think. *Maybe I should be doing more to find someone.*

But really, my plight could be worse. I have a friend whose mom asked him if he's gay because he hasn't been dating. Camerin and I both have heard of similar stories about relatives questioning a single's sexual preference. How can we prove to our families that it's OK that we're single and not constantly on the prowl? Isn't the latter a good thing? And how do we deal with this confusion that doesn't only hit close to home . . . but comes from home?

I had to face these doubts head-on at a cousin's wedding. Long ago, married people got together and decided that it wasn't enough to have big celebrations to announce their marriages, but they had to go the extra mile and turn it into a *complete* harassment of those still single. The answer? The bouquet and garter toss. "Let's get them all gathered in front of everyone and watch them squirm!"

At this particular wedding, I couldn't handle the ritual or the questions about why I wasn't seeing anyone, so I excused myself to the restroom during that portion of the reception. When I returned, I faced questions anyway. So, I handled it the best way I could. I flipped the table like Jesus in the temple and used a chair as a battering ram to get to the door. Well, OK, I just went for the whole honesty-is-the-best-policy thing. I told them I was uncomfortable with assumptions that I should have a girlfriend or a wife. "God is using me in my single state right now," I explained, "and I'm OK with it. And while I want to marry one day and try to meet someone, I think singleness can be as much of a ministry as marriage." Amazingly, this worked!

This started lots of honesty in my family about being single. My sister now prays about my singleness. She prays that God will send me a wife, or, if that's not in his will, she asks him to use me, support me, and keep me content where I am in life. I can think of no better prayer for my family members to say for my single days—no matter how many of them there may be.

TECHNO TRENDS

Camerin: I've always thought there's something altogether strange about trying to find love in a techno age. I've often joked about the inevitable outcome: telling my grandkids someday, "Then your grandfather IMed me, and the rest is history." Hmm. Not exactly the kind of love story singles dream of. Technological means of meeting and getting to know a date—email, the Internet, search engines, cell phones, text messaging, etc.—seem impersonal. And yet, in a day when dates are often hard to come by, they provide new, creative means for making a love connection (more on this in chapters 7 and 8). So we've come to a place in dating history when I sometimes read personal ads with my friends for sport, when 72 percent of ChristianSinglesToday.com readers admit to doing a Google search on a crush (out of 857 respondents), and when I hardly know how to interact with a new love interest without the use of email.

In fact, email has become so widespread in relationshipdom that none of us even batted an eye when romantic flick faves Meg Ryan and Tom Hanks used it to find love in *You've Got Mail*. While that movie portrayed the good aspects of email interactions—namely getting to know someone's personality before looks and hormones can factor in—it also showed the inherent complexities. Things written in an email can be misconstrued, no matter how many emoticons we add to try to convey the things we usually communicate with vocal inflection and body language. With email you have time to think about what you want to write, and you can read the messages on your own timetable and in the comfort of your own home (and pj's). But in person, you must sustain real-time conversation. You must think on your feet. And usually, if you're out in public at least, you have to wear shoes.

I admit that more than once I've used email to initiate a conversation with a guy I'm interested in. Usually I find an excuse to send the guy a quick, breezy message—and, really, an email address is an easy thing to access. Luckily these guys have emailed me back, and we've enjoyed a techno chat back and forth until we've eventually transitioned to the coveted in-person meeting.

But before that three-dimensional get-together, there are countless questions about email etiquette that leave us singles perplexed. Should I explain how I got the guy's email address? How soon is too soon to respond? To smiley face or not to smiley face? If you have the same Internet service provider, is it too forward to instant message the person? And the mother of all email conundrums: will email chemistry translate to in-person chemistry?

With the advent of easy access to anyone, anywhere, anytime—and in our fast-food, ATM culture—we've also become accustomed to quickness. The arena of relationships is no exception. Enter speed dating. If you aren't familiar with this newish meet-and-greet trend, let me inform you. Basically, a group of women sits in a big circle around the same number of men and chats with the person in front of them for three to eight minutes (depending on the host organization's setup) and then rotates to the next mini "date." Sounds wacky, until you learn that a Jewish rabbi came up with the idea as a way to help the single members of his flock mix and mingle and date only within the faith. I was skeptical, until I had to try it for an article I was assigned to write. It was a fun adventure, but it didn't yield a ton of results (more on this in chapter 8). At least not for me. One of my friends met a guy there whom she dated for a whole year. Go figure!

It's the same with Internet dating services. I met the last two guys I dated through eHarmony, a truth I was embarrassed to admit at first. When I was dating the first of the two and people asked how we met, I usually lowered my voice and got a sheepish look on my face as I said, "Through the Internet." As embarrassed as I was to admit it, no one else seemed fazed in the least. In fact, when my *grandfather* suggested I sign up for an Internet dating service, I knew much of the stigma was gone.

But questions about the effectiveness remained. Is this really a viable means for meeting a mate? Are all those commercials and magazine ads with happy-looking couples who met on the Web accurate—or are these folks the lucky few? Can you really find lasting love on the same medium where you can buy out-of-print books, find driving directions, locate long-lost high school classmates, and access porn? Well, yes and no. I have friends who've been with a service for a whole year with no luck. And to be honest, it's left them poorer (some of these services aren't cheap!) and with a shakier self-esteem (as in, "Why isn't this working for *me?*"). But, as with speed dating, just when you want to write it off as ridiculous, you witness a success story. During the time Todd and I were writing this book, a good friend of mine got engaged to a great guy she met online. (More on Internet dating in chapter 7.) When you hear a story like that, you realize God can use any method to match up his kids.

While God can get pretty creative as he writes people's love stories, he also gave us intelligence and common sense as we consider dating options. So how much skepticism and how much optimism do you bring to speed dating, Internet dating services, and to the next dating trend that's sure to follow? Again, more questions and confusion about the current State of the Date.

2

The Dating Drought

Why Aren't Christian Singles Dating?

Camerin: I was sitting in a trendy Cuban restaurant, enjoying a Friday night dinner with my friend Noelle, when I fully grasped the negative consequences all the confusion outlined in chapter 1 has had on singles. "How do they all do it?" Noelle asked as she motioned to the couples around us, obviously on dates. They, no doubt, had been drawn to the restaurant's romantic atmosphere. We, on the other hand, had been drawn there by the yummy entrees that accommodated Noelle's recent conversion to a low-carb diet.

I knew exactly what Noelle, a fellow never-married thirtysome-thing, was getting at. We were a deserted island of single dateless-ness in a sea of coupledom. Again.

We compared notes about the months, nay years, since our last date. And when we recounted the social lives (or lack thereof) of our other single female friends, we saw a depressing pattern emerge.

I looked across the table at Noelle, a college professor, a strong woman of faith, and a petite, blue-eyed brunette, and thought, *If she can't get a date, we're all doomed!*

As much as I know singleness is about so much more than dating—and dating about more than qualifications and looks—I was troubled by what appeared to be a dating dearth. But what really clinched this as a full-on trend was when I addressed this topic in my singles column and received more than 250 emails from singles across the country pouring out their frustrated, heartbroken, or simply perplexed stories of datelessness. An informal poll taken on the site shortly thereafter revealed that 54 percent of 671 single respondents hadn't been on a date in more than two years.

While I was comforted that my friends and I weren't trapped in some odd dateless vortex, I was disturbed by one vexing question: *why?* In a society in which singles make up 43 percent of U.S. residents 15 and over (according to the U.S. Census Bureau) and in which most of the singles I know desire to be married at some point, why are so many of us having such a difficult time getting a date?

WHATCHOO TALKIN' ABOUT, WILLIS?

TODD: But before we get too far into why there's a dating drought, I want to look at why it matters. Obviously, some Christians don't believe in dating. Others are going to ask, "Is it really a *bad* thing that Christians aren't dating?"

Before we can answer that, we have to address another question: when we use the word *dating*, what are we talking about? Well, I don't mean casual dating just to have fun. And I don't even necessarily mean "guy sees girl, guy asks girl out, guy picks her up at 7:00 on Friday" dating. Instead, I define dating as a purposeful, God-directed process of getting to know someone to build a romantic relationship. This could start by a stranger asking out someone he noticed from across a crowded room. This could start with a DTR (Define the Relationship) chat after several months or years of friendship. But I believe it all needs to be coated in prayer, directed at eventually finding a spouse, and done with a godly love for the other person.

Of course, dating isn't everyone's choice. Whether it's a personal conviction or just part of taking a break from relationships, I understand the concept of not dating. And that's not the sort of "Christians aren't dating" we're concerned about. We're not debating the question "Should we date or not?" Either answer to that question is a valid choice God can use. But both Camerin and I personally believe in dating. Both of us practice it—well, not with each other. (We believe we're called to friendship. We'll talk more about intergender friendship in chapter 13.) Who we want to speak to in this book are Christians who wish they were dating to find a God-approved spouse, but aren't. When Christians want to date but are forced into a long-term romantic drought, there are going to be some negative side effects.

Working for ChristianSinglesToday.com, Camerin has seen a lot of emails from singles who have the God-given desire to love a spouse and raise a family but haven't had a romantic interest in years. Some look around and see no possible love interests. Others have been burnt by rejections, denial, and years of seemingly no interest from the opposite gender. This all adds up to bad by-products, including bitterness and clouded thinking. In addition, a shortage of dating experience or apparent options of dating can in some cases lead to settling for Mr./Ms. Close Enough. Or we can become so jaded we make generalizations and assumptions about the other gender as a whole. These false impressions only extend the gap of misunderstanding about two genders who sometimes can misunderstand each other in big ways. I can't tell you how many times I've heard, "[Men or women] just don't understand us/aren't doing enough/have too high of expectations!" But we'll get to all these things more in later chapters.

WIDESPREAD PAIN

Camerin: When I started to see a recurring theme of undesired datelessness in the emails I received from singles who read my column, I was struck by several things: the length of some people's dating drought, the confusion as to how they got there, and the intensity of the resulting pain and frustration. When such emails numbered into the hundreds, I realized how widespread this issue is. And when I read the heartbroken contents therein, I realized how deep this issue strikes the hearts of those affected by it. Here's just a small sampling of these troubling messages:

> I've been a committed Christian single all of my life. At sixteen I chose to commit my love life to God; at forty-eight I'm still waiting for a husband.
>
> I didn't date much as a teenager because there were few Christian boys to date in my small Midwest high school, and I only wanted to date Christians. During my college years I attended a church that believed singles shouldn't date. Those who chose to marry were supposed to discern God's choice for a marriage partner by just hanging out in groups. After leaving this church, I had my first serious boyfriend, and we became engaged. This man was supposedly a Christian, but he wound up sexually involved with another woman. I broke up with him, and I was devastated.

34

I moved to another part of the country and became involved in a megachurch with many singles. This church also taught against dating and encouraged singles to hang out in groups and "hear from God" about who to marry. During this time, I was told two conflicting lies. The first lie was that I wasn't married because I didn't have enough faith. I was supposed to just wait for a man to pursue me, even though none of the men I knew were taking the initiative to do that. I was in my midtwenties by this time, and my biological clock was ticking. I wanted to get married and have children, but it wasn't happening. When I expressed my desires to Christian leaders, I was told the second lie: you're not married because marriage is an idol to you. I was made to feel that my desire for marriage and children was sinful.

At thirty-two, I joined a church-planting team. In this new church, marriage, children, and homeschooling were glorified, whereas singles were subservient and devalued. I eventually left this church, and I now refuse to be a part of any other church that teaches against dating. How are you to choose a good marriage partner if you don't take time to date and get to know a potential partner?

I was told to be sexually pure and prepare for marriage and motherhood my whole life. But I was never told what to do when that doesn't happen. I'm angry that I was lied to and manipulated by Christian leaders during my most marriageable years, and that now, at forty-eight, even if I do marry, I'll never have children. I feel deeply disappointed with God about this.

S.B.

I was very busy in my twenties with a good job and a fulfilling ministry with junior high and high school students. I sought the Lord about marriage at age twenty-one and concluded it was for me. Silly me, I assumed my wife would turn up long before I hit thirty. When she hadn't shown up by then and I looked around at who was now available for a deeper relationship, it was like going mansion shopping in East St. Louis.

I've dated a few women over the last few years, only to have them decide I'm good simply for friendship. I've noticed in several church circles that there's so much emphasis put on Jesus Christ being the focus of every part of your life that any sort of romance seems squeezed out of the picture. As a result, singles seem to want to have godly friends as long as the friends of the opposite gender don't go further than a friendship. But if a guy has a lot of money or a woman has a hot body, then the attitude is, "That person is mine, and I'll deal with his/her lack of character later." I'm not implying that

rich hunks and gorgeous babes will always
be against God. But the world's standards
of what's valuable in a mate seem to have
become the church's standard as well. I'm
convinced this is a primary reason for the
ridiculously high divorce rate.

name withheld

It seems to me that if you're in your
twenties, dating isn't too much of a
problem. The older one gets, there seems
to be a decline in opportunities. As
for me, I'm almost forty and have never
dated. Yep, that's right. When I was in
my twenties, I thought dating and getting
married would happen naturally in the
course of life. Little did I know then
that I'd now be fast approaching forty
with no dating prospects period.

But I still feel somewhat like a freak
for being this age and never having gone
on a date. At this stage in my life, it's
even hard to get together with friends on
the weekend. Most are too busy or have
moved out of state.

I'm beginning to wonder how much
God really interacts in all this. Even
though I might sound negative, I still
would rather remain single than be in a
relationship that should never have taken
place. At this point I don't think I'll
ever get married. Such is life, I guess.

Sheri

37

I've been single-again for almost three
and a half years, and I've been on a total
of three dates in that time. As a former
swimsuit model, I don't believe I'm the
most unattractive woman in the world. But
it's amazing, and frustrating, to me that
there aren't more quality Christian single
men who are willing to ask out healthy,
well-balanced, God-fearing women. I truly
believe in the supportive wife role, which
I'd think a man would be attracted to. I'm
glad I'm not the only one having a problem
finding a quality Christian man to date. I
was beginning to think something was wrong
with me!

M.M.

My "love life" as a single Christian
woman has been full of disappointments. I
went through a season of believing there
were no good Christian men left. All of
the Christian guys I knew pursued new
Christians or non-Christians. They skipped
over me, a committed church volunteer who
grew up in the church. Did that make me
overqualified?

In college, the Christian guys on
my campus dated my closest friends but
skipped over me. Years later, I discovered
they felt they weren't good enough for me.
I held high positions with our college
magazine and somehow maintained a 3.8
grade-point average. I also helped start

a Bible study in my dorm. By the time I graduated college, I'd already purchased my own town home, had a great job, and was even doing some runway modeling. I could tell you how to run a company but couldn't even tell you how it felt to hold hands with a guy.

There was a guy at my church who showed interest in me but never told me. He told my pastor, my sister, and my friends. He believed God told him I was to be his wife. But the guy never even asked me out.

I didn't go on my first date until I was almost twenty-three years old. Two months before my birthday, I started dating a really nice guy who had become a good friend of mine. I finally had my first kiss, my first boyfriend, and my first chance to go to the movies with a person other than family or friends. But nine months into the relationship, the guy disclosed that he'd been fudging the truth about his religious beliefs. Although he helped me memorize Scriptures and talked about the Bible and God and his church, he wasn't a Christian. He was afraid to tell me because he didn't want me to leave him.

I dated him for two years, and although we broke up because we finally had to face the reality of being unequally yoked, we're still pals.

I talk to the guys I come in contact with. I have several brothers and hang out with them and their friends. I even strike up conversations with the guys about movies I want to see or concerts coming

39

to town. I enjoy football, attend Super
Bowl parties, and even play scrimmage
basketball with the guys. I admit I've
never asked a guy out, but that's because
I feel that if I take that step, I may
seem desperate. And I don't want to take
the "leadership" role, because I like for
guys to take control.

But the Christian guys who know me know
that I'm twenty-six years old and own my
own home, my own car, hold a managerial
position at work, travel all over the
country, and love God with a passion. What
they don't know is that the non-Christian
who asked me out is the only guy to ever
ask for my phone number in twenty-six
years.

Where did I go wrong?

D.

WHERE DO WE GO FROM HERE?

Camerin: While it's obvious many factors (some unpacked in chapter 1) have contributed to the current dating drought in Christian
circles, what's tougher to discern is how to move forward. Personally,
discovering I wasn't the only one dateless in Christianville was a huge
relief. It helped me see that my sometimes wide-open social calendar
wasn't necessarily due to the fact that men had somehow deemed me
not date-worthy. But it didn't mean I was off the hook. Just because
the issue isn't necessarily internal doesn't mean there aren't steps I
need to take if I sincerely desire to be in a relationship.

I got a peek at a potential solution to the dating drought when
a single friend begged me to sign up for a Christian online dating

service with her last January on a spontaneous New Year's resolution whim. Within two months we each found ourselves in a dating relationship with a great Christian guy. Similarly, a mutual friend of ours had a year-long dating relationship with a man she met at a speed dating event. While there are still pitfalls and needed cautions with these trendy new ways to find love, they're fast becoming the new "normal." Current stats show that 45 million people log on to online dating services each month. While these stories aren't exactly what you dream of telling your grandkids someday, they sure beat the possibility of not having grandkids. We'll talk more about the pluses and pitfalls of Internet dating in chapter 7.

Rutgers University's 2003 National Marriage Project speaks to the troubling effect divorce has had on those who grew up in the seventies and eighties, asserting that many singles today are "more insecure about relationships, and more likely to experience a divorce themselves." Yet not all current statistics are worrisome. The median age for first-time marriage for women is up from twenty in 1960 to the current age of twenty-five, and for men is up from twenty-two in 1960 to twenty-seven. The results of this slower pace to the altar apparently are healthy. According to the Rutgers marriage study, "The increase in the median age at first marriage appears to have had a strongly positive effect. One recent study by a prominent demographer has found it to be by far the single most important factor accounting for the recent leveling off of divorce rates."[3]

When I look around at my cool Christian friends who are still single and dateless, and *still* receive heartfelt emails about my "Why Aren't Christians Dating?" column from last year, I hope and pray these new stats are a glimpse at a better, healthier trend to come.

EVERYTHING I LEARNED IN KINDERGARTEN . . .

TODD: It's funny to me how things have changed. I remember spending my kindergarten recesses chasing around Julie Elliot, the cutest girl in our class. All the boys did it. Somehow, it was just the thing to do: you ran after her, and she ran away. We didn't know why we were doing it, and I sure never thought about what I'd do if I caught her (which I didn't, because Julie was both really cute *and* really fast).

This is funny to me now because back then we chased girls without thinking about it—and without knowing why. Now, we think about it too much, know why we would do it, but have quit all the chasing and running. Instead, both genders seem to be standing on opposite sides of the playground, making the same kinds of judgments against each other. "*They* don't do this," or "*They* think this." Meanwhile, nobody is crossing the kickball field to talk to each other.

We just wait for each other to either start running or chasing. And like all things since those days in kindergarten, the situation has gotten awfully complex. In the next few chapters, Camerin and I want to try and unpack some of these complexities: a lack of men in the church, changing gender roles, and the question of who should be asking out whom anyway.

3

Men in the Church

O Brother, Where Art Thou?

Camerin: Something's broken. I don't exactly know what it is or how to fix it, which maddens me to no end. I just know that something's unmistakably Not Right.

You see, recently I was at a conference for people who run Christian magazines for women in Eastern Europe. We had nearly all the countries that end in "ia" represented: Russia, Bulgaria, Lithuania, Slovakia, Romania, Croatia, Serbia, and the like. I, ever the lover of people from other cultures, was in heaven. At every meal or coffee break or evening playtime I was able to ask one of my favorite questions: "What's life like in your corner of the world?"

It was a recurring answer to a cousin of this favorite question—"What are the main things your magazine's readers wrestle with?"—that most disturbed me. It points to a singleness issue I've seen too often. Now, I swear I didn't tell any of these women I'm a singles columnist. Some of them didn't even know I'm single, that I'm a never-married thirtysomething with countless female friends in the same boat (or even slightly older boats).

The first such conversation at the conference, with a lovely fortysomething woman from Russia, went something like this:

Me: "So what are the main things Christian women in Russia wrestle with?"

Galina: "We have many smart, wonderful girls who are single in our churches. But no men for them."

Me (my voice a mixture of empathy and depression): "Really?"

Galina: "Yes. Is quite sad. Many are going to United States to find husband."

Me (all sweetness and cultural sensitivity): "Well, tell them to get in line!"

Next it was a conversation with the two Bulgarians who'd put a single thirty-four-year-old woman on the cover of their magazine because the growing group of single women in their country faces big pressures to wed and to put life on hold until marriage. This particular single woman was setting a good example by leading a big, full life. As we talked about the challenges such women face, they painted a similar picture of a plethora of Christian women without the same number of Christian male counterparts.

The next day at lunch when someone asked me if I had any children and I answered, "No, I'm not married," the never-married thirty-eight-year-old Greek woman next to me blurted, "Oh, that makes me feel so much better!" She, too, shared about the seemingly missing generation of single men in her home country. As did a Malaysian woman who hadn't married until twenty-nine, an "old" age in her culture.

While there was a little part of me that enjoyed this kinship and understanding of my reality, I also was depressed that this apparent inequity in the singleness gender ratio is *global*. As I said, something's broken here.

A CAVEAT

Camerin: Now, before all the guys slam this book down in indignation, let me say I do know there are godly single men in our world. I'm well aware. I'm great friends with some of them and have dated a few others. And yes, there are certainly pockets where the gender split is fifty-fifty or even skewed to the male side (if you could let me know where those churches are, that'd be great!). I even attended one such church (the fifty-fifty kind) during a recent business trip.

My contention is simply that on the whole there appear to be so many less single men in Christian circles than there are single women. My own experience has borne this truth out. Nearly all the church groups, Bible studies, singles groups, and Christian workplaces I've been a part of over the years have been populated by lots of single women and noticeably (and frustratingly) less single men. My current crop of single friends is mostly comprised of godly women.

I kid you not, when I was in InterVarsity Christian Fellowship at the secular university I attended years ago, one of our recurring prayer requests was for more men to join our community (for their benefit as well as for ours!). A male co-worker recently told me about a college visit he made with his teenage daughter. Apparently she ruled out the Christian campus they were checking out when she discovered the female-to-male ratio is two-to-one. Sadly, this isn't an uncommon phenomenon for Christian colleges.

Every time the company newsletter comes out at the Christian office where I work, there's a laundry list of new single female employees. In stark contrast, I could count the single men in our company practically on one hand—out of a company of 150 workers!

I often joke with Todd that because of his gender, he's got a buffet of dating/mate choices stretched out before him. I, on the other hand, I lament with great drama, am starving in the desert.

NOT BUYING IT

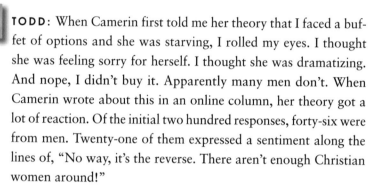

TODD: When Camerin first told me her theory that I faced a buffet of options and she was starving, I rolled my eyes. I thought she was feeling sorry for herself. I thought she was dramatizing. And nope, I didn't buy it. Apparently many men don't. When Camerin wrote about this in an online column, her theory got a lot of reaction. Of the initial two hundred responses, forty-six were from men. Twenty-one of them expressed a sentiment along the lines of, "No way, it's the reverse. There aren't enough Christian women around!"

I can relate. The church I grew up in, a small, rural town I still visit on occasion when I go home to see my parents, has at least five single men in their thirties and forties and no regularly attending single women of the same age group. I also used to attend a Bible study with an even ratio of single men and women. So I never noticed a deficiency of men. In fact, the youth group I volunteer with at my church—made up of both junior high and high school students—is strongly male-heavy. That's why I thought Camerin was wrong. But then I looked at the research. In 2000, the Barna Research Group found in a nationwide survey that 60 percent of adherents to Christianity are women. The survey also looked at the number of each gender whose beliefs identified them as born-again Christians. Based on the results, Barna estimates there are currently between eleven million and thirteen million more born-again women than born-again men in the U.S.

But what's startling is not just the gender disparity among Christian adherents; it's also the difference between men who believe and those who are active in their belief. Although 36 percent of men in the Barna survey were identified as born-again believers, only 14 percent attend Sunday school, 13 percent belong to a small group, and 9 percent have held any leadership position in a church. Each category's percentages were substantially higher for women.[4]

This forced me to honestly reconsider what I've seen. I'm the only regularly attending single man between 25 and 45 at my good-sized church. Working for a Christian business has been the most eye-opening. Like Camerin mentioned, there're 5 or 6 single men in our office, and I can count at least 3 times that amount of single women. And then there're all the emails. Camerin has received letters from women troubled by the absence of single Christian men for a long time, but when she first wrote on it the floodgates opened. While 21 of those initial 46 men disagreed with Camerin, 25 agreed. But of all the women (more than 150) who wrote in, not one disagreed with her. These women tell such detailed and convincing stories that I can't deny it any longer. There are less single men than women active in the church, and depending on where you are, the difference can be staggering. Sure, as I've seen, this isn't true everywhere. Rural areas, sections of the country near military bases, and ministries with strong male leaders are particularly likely to have equal numbers or even more men. But far more common are stories like Margaret's:

> Since becoming a Christian, I've been on zero dates. I simply don't get asked out. Why? Because our churches and Christian circles are full of women and are horribly void of single, eligible men. No matter

47

where I go—Bible studies, church, singles groups—it is 90 percent female.

GOOD NEWS, BAD NEWS

TODD: You'd think the presence of more Christian single women would be like winning the lottery for men (90 percent women! It's like a dream!). But I think there's possible bad news too. In fact, two troubling ideas for men extend from this disparity.

One single guy who wrote to ChristianSinglesToday.com best states the first negative. He wrote:

> At least women can blame demographics for being single. Here I am, single at twenty-nine and unable to get the time of day from any of those women outnumbering me two to one. The marriage game is stacked in my favor, and I'm still unable to find just one! That amounts to a real blow to one's self-esteem. I get that dismissal from people at church all the time: "What's wrong with you? The church is full of women!"

One of the most common worries in singledom is simply, "*Is there something wrong with me?*" And for guys, the idea that we're outnumbered but still looking might mean: *Yup, there* is *something wrong with us.* We don't want to admit we have an advantage because of what that could say about us. I look back at my eye rolls when first learning about the gender disparity and realize I was feeling attacked. It was like confirmation that there's so much wrong with me that I'm still single, even with a head start. It's a

48

lot like when I play basketball with my youth group kids. I blame my losses on anything I can: I'm getting old, I'm just a little out of shape, I don't practice enough, or the sun is in my eyes. Anything is better than just admitting I suck at basketball.

The other troubling thought is that maybe women aren't really attracted to me for who I am but because I'm a rare and interested single male Christian who has a pulse. Just like women, I want to be valued for who I am. I want a woman who sees I have something to offer as a husband and a partner. I want a woman to love me for me, not because I could be her only chance for a family. A friend of mine recently met a slightly older Christian woman whom he really liked. They got along great for a few months. It seemed the relationship was headed places until she told him one day that she wasn't attracted to him. She'd known it all along but was hesitant to break up with him because it felt nice to have someone doting on her after nearly ten years without any romantic interest. That clearly isn't what men or women want in a relationship.

THE FAITHFUL FEW?

TODD: Yes, the lack of single men in our churches is bad for the whole dating equation. But obviously that's not the biggest problem. The biggest problem is that single men aren't in our churches. In fact, men in general seem less interested than women in spiritual things. The 2000 survey by the Barna Research Group revealed that 75 percent of women said their religious faith is very important in their life. Only 60 percent of men said the same.

Frankly, I'm worried about my Christian brothers and male seekers. Is faith typically less important to men? Why are we less active in our faith? Is a relationship with our Creator really contingent on our gender?

Well, of course I don't think women have a special "God gene." Like Camerin said, something is broken. And I don't think it's something easy to pinpoint—or even that it's just *one* broken thing. I think there are faulty cracks all over the place, including in cultural gender roles, societal expectations, and the setup of the church. John Eldredge aptly hit the nail on the head in his book *Wild at Heart*:

> Society at large can't make up its mind about men. Having spent the last thirty years redefining masculinity into something more sensitive, safe, manageable and, well, feminine, it now berates men for not being men. Boys will be boys, they sigh. As though if a man were to really grow up he would forsake wilderness and wanderlust and settle down, be at home forever in Aunt Polly's parlor. "Where are the *real* men?" is regular fare for talk shows and new books. *You asked them to be women*, I want to say. The result is a gender confusion never experienced at such a wide level in the history of the world. . . . And then, alas, there is the church. . . . I think most men in the church believe that God put them on the earth to be a good boy. The problem with men, we are told, is that they don't know how to keep their promises, be spiritual leaders, talk to their wives, or raise their children. But if they try real hard they can reach the lofty summit of becoming . . . a nice guy. That's what we hold up as models of Christian maturity: Really Nice Guys.[5]

Men commonly just don't know what or who we're supposed to be. Mixed messages and gender confusion can particularly screw up us younger, single men. Without clear guidance, it's easy to follow the wrong way. Even though our culture can't really decide how it wants its men, there are some definite revered qualities: promiscuity, hedonism, self-reliance, and looking out for number one. And all of these can look like more enticing options than what guys see in the church—pressure to just be quiet and nice.

Think of culture and Christianity as two storefronts next to each other on the street. Both have signs advertising their offerings. Culture advertises sex, recklessness, alcohol, instant gratification, and not having to rely on anybody but yourself. On the other hand, the church window seems to promise judgment, rules, and hymns. As an extra bonus, there's a family focus and a largely feminine, touchy-feely outlook. Looking at it this way, it's a little more understandable why many men leave the church after high school and come back only as married men with families, a shifted focus, and a greater emotional maturity, if they come back at all. They've sown their wild oats, seen the errors of their ways, and now understand what's truly lasting and important in life.

A lot of men also claim to stay away from the church because of pressure to be something they're not: married.

Here's what one single guy told Britain's *Christianity and Renewal*:

```
    Maybe part of the problem lies in
the kind of church we're being asked to
join. Accepting Jesus might be an easier
proposition if it didn't mean accepting
a wife, family, [and a] Labrador. If
the moment a man sets his foot through
the door he is laden with a bundle of
expectations and pressures he is hardly
likely to stay around for long. The older
the single man gets, the heavier the
expectation. Why? Because we have taken
one choice and turned it into the only
choice. What is needed, I think, is for
the church to turn the pressure off.
Instead of seeing young men as potential
husbands and fathers, maybe we should
start by seeing them as human beings.
```

OK, so things don't look good here. There's no magic switch to immediately open up the man floodgates in church. I admit the

problem with a lack of men active in the church can look daunting. Guys in the church can think, *Well, if I'm the only one here
... then, why am I here?* And women may just throw in the towel
and head for the convent, or for non-Christians (which we'll get
to in chapter 5).

But while an overview of this cultural trend looks bleak, I think
there's hope.

BEING ALL WE CAN BE

TODD: Basically, I think the hope lies not in concentrating on
the big picture but in focusing on our individual faith. Each of us
men needs to focus on strengthening our walks, finding a mentor,
and becoming active in the local church. A side effect this ideally
would have is to show an example to other men, which perhaps
could help balance the gender picture in churches. But regardless
of the dating picture or even how churches look at singles, we men
need to set a standard of living for God.

Samantha, a ChristianSinglesToday.com reader, put it well when
she wrote,

> It's not the responsibility of the
> women to try and get more men in church
> so we can date them. Each person needs to
> take personal responsibility for his own
> relationship with God—you can't blame the
> church. It fumes me that men skip church
> or ministries because they say it doesn't
> challenge them or that it isn't fun for
> them. We all need to be in fellowship, and
> that's a personal decision.

A friend of mine and I were talking recently about our own faiths. We both work at Christian companies and revealed to each other that we fear that if we were ever to go back to secular organizations, our convictions would falter and we'd slip back into less-committed versions of ourselves. That made me realize that a real key to strengthening faith is community. Whether it be through small groups, intimate fellowship, or just an active role in our local church, Christian community (supplemented by private quiet time with God) teaches us how to live out this faith of ours in practical ways.

The men I work with at Christianity Today International have not only taught me a lot about relationships, God, and career, but have also shown me what godly men look like. When I started there, I quickly saw that I didn't live my life to their standard. They were an inspiration to me with their care for one another, discipline, and daily surrender to God's will.

Thinking about this aspect of my personal journey reminded me of one of the first things Jesus often said to new disciples. He'd say, "You know, this is gonna be hard. You up for it?" Few guys will deny that kind of invitation, because we want challenges. We see this same lesson from the U.S. military. When facing a dip in recruits after Vietnam, the Army lowered their expectations. The Marines heightened theirs. Guess who saw its numbers rise? I think we can expect the same if we Christian men stand up, set the bar high, and encourage those around us to live up to it.

What's the expectation we should set for men? Well, like Eldredge says, it's not to be a "nice guy." And it's not that once you walk in the church your focus should be on starting a family. Instead, the expectation should be to follow God's flesh-and-blood model for what a man should be. And I don't mean the softly painted, smiling Jesus with children and sheep at his feet that we often see. Instead, we should look at the full picture: the Jesus who wept, who got angry, who took risks, who encouraged others to risk it all, who told people what he thought, who rubbed mud and spit on people's faces, and who just showed love. The complete Jesus of the Bible is a real man—a well-rounded, complete man—who sets the ultimate standard for being all we can be.

WHAT WOMEN CAN DO

Camerin: When I was at that international conference making the discovery that the shortage of single Christian men is global, I prayed silently after one such conversation: "God, you obviously are revealing a trend to me. But please don't leave me there. I don't want to just sit with this knowledge and become frustrated. I need action steps. I want something to do with this information." So, I'm doing what I know to do: I'm writing about it. Sounding the alarm, so to speak, that something's wrong. Pleading with our churches to target this missing demographic. And praying, as I've been doing since that conference a few weeks ago, for revival among the single men of this world.

I think prayer is one of the best things women can do about this trend. One woman who responded to my column about the man-shortage put it so eloquently: "My prayer today is that we as women of God begin to pray for our men like never before, not out of selfish motivation but out of a sincere place of longing for our brothers to take their rightful places in church, in ministry, and maybe, just maybe, in our hearts."

Along with the knowledge of seeming brokenness in our world, there's one thing I know for sure that gives me hope. Our God specializes in broken things, in crafting something from nothing, in creating beauty from ashes. You and I are living proof. And hopefully, with his grace, we'll see him work such wondrous miracles again in this arena.

4

Changing Gender Roles

You've Come a Long Way, Baby?

Camerin: Recently I gratefully watched my friend Tim install my mondo-heavy window-unit air conditioner. He hefted; I moved things out of his way. He wielded his cordless screwdriver; I stood by in silent tool envy. He wedged a block of wood in the window as a final securing touch; I clapped my admiration and appreciation.

I relay this story to show that I *can* accept help from the male of the species. Really. I also share this as exhibit A in my case of confusion over being labeled "too independent" by several other males of the species. I've heard this specific accusation from male friends of mine, and I've also been a general recipient of this indictment from male readers of my singles column who write in to complain about women being "too independent these days."

Too independent? In some ways that seems like a contradiction to me. Like being too tidy or too happy. What's so wrong with it? Aren't there a gazillion worse things to be "too much" of?

I'll admit that more than a decade of having to fend for myself as an adult has prompted me to meet a few offers of "Can I help you with that?" with a confident, "No thanks, I've got it." Though I can't expect the polite offerers to know this, my main motivation for that response is more habit than raging independence. I'm just used to hefting, schlepping, opening, and fixing things for myself. And I'm trying to step back and graciously accept these offers more often than not.

I also recognize that women's roles have shifted markedly over the past generation or two. In my parents' generation, most women went right from their father's home to their husband's home. Mere decades ago, women's financial, professional, relational, and political security rested mainly in the hands of their husband. I often forget that my ability to have a career and ministry pursuits, an existence several states away from my parents, my own car and solo apartment, my own bank account and 401K are largely new freedoms.

It stands to reason that all these changes and advances have affected the way men and women relate to one another. Some women say men are intimidated by the strides we've made as a gender, by the new-and-improved modern woman who enters relationships with education, financial freedom, work experience, and, yes, independence to offer. Instead of their being intimidated, I'd like to think (or at least hope) that men are simply confused about how to relate to us in these changing roles—or, more likely, a combination of both.

A CATCH-22

Camerin: Ironically, the dating dearth and postponement of marriage that surely are somewhat related to this new gender-role confusion have forced me and my female counterparts to be even more independent. Not always because we want to be, but sometimes because we have to be. It's not like we went out and got jobs (and cars and condos) to make men obsolete in our lives. No, like our male counterparts, we went to school to invest in our interests and God-given talents and then set out to use that education to find fulfillment, to bless others, to stretch our minds, to hopefully bring glory to God, and more often than not, simply to pay the rent!

As a never-married thirtysomething, I'm not going to sit back and let everything from my finances to my temperamental toilet go untended. I'm going to learn these new skills, make advancements in my career, buy my own car and condo, invest in a retirement plan. Putting life on hold until marriage isn't a good or God-honoring option.

Plus, I'd like to think these strides, skills, and accomplishments are good things when it comes to romantic relationships. Look at all the extra benefits my female counterparts and I bring to the table now. Men don't have to carry the weight of our security and identity anymore. Surely that's a welcome relief.

But instead of being seen as more well-rounded and less needy, often I'm just called too independent. And I'm not even exactly sure what that means. Am I supposed to still be living at home? Am I supposed to leave stuff around my apartment in a state of disrepair instead of going in search of my wrench or duct tape? Am I supposed to pass up a church leadership opportunity so that a man can fill it instead? What does a "just right" level of independence look like?

Just because I do many things for myself doesn't mean I wouldn't gladly step aside and let a man do some of these things for me. I recognize there are things men are, on average, better at than women. I welcome their skills, abilities, know-how, strength, and intelligence. In fact, I'd be their biggest cheerleader and admirer in these things if we could simply find a way to come together and become a mutually beneficial "we."

Even if I would go so far as to say I don't need a man, wouldn't it be enough that I still *want* one in my life? Isn't a peer better than a "cling-on"? Isn't it a good thing that women now come with financial independence, careers, and possibly even a few power tools?

At times I suspect "women are too independent" is a cop-out for men, much in the same way "men are intimidated by modern women" is for women. While there are probably kernels of truth in both statements, neither comes close to acknowledging the sociological, demographical, and relational changes afoot when it comes to gender roles. Maybe it's time we all dropped our excuses, however valid they may be, and together try to navigate a new, healthy way for men and women to relate to one another.

So here I am admitting I need help. I need the men who are wary of women's changing roles to even consider it a good thing that we bring more to the table in relationships these days. I need the women who take these new freedoms to the extreme and who live by an "I don't need no man" attitude to rethink how you view our brothers.

Mostly, I need God's help to know how to navigate these tricky waters, how to respect others even in the midst of frustration, when to be strong and when to lean on others, when to stride ahead and when to stand back and applaud the menfolk in my life.

DO THE ACCUSATIONS MAKE SENSE?

TODD: I've noticed an interesting difference between my male and female friends over the past four years of owning a pickup truck. In that time, only one guy friend has ever asked me to help him move anything. But for female friends, I've moved multiple beds, moving boxes, couches, bikes, etc. . . . I'm always happy to help women. In fact, I may get business cards printed up saying: "Todd Hertz, Carrier of Heavy Stuff for Single Ladies."

OK, seriously, do a few instances of hauling stuff *really* say anything about the state of single women's independence? Not really. It shows that my female friends aren't afraid to ask when they need help; however, I don't think it proves the attitude of an entire gender. The same could be said of the evidence used by people who argue women are too independent. Not only does the criticism not fit an entire gender, but I think the entire premise of the argument is faulty. Just because a woman has a successful career, we assume she chose career over marriage? Just because a woman learns to get by on her own, men cite her for being too strong to want a husband or even a dating partner?

Here are some arguments from ChristianSinglesToday.com readers:

> Women have become lovers of self and may not see the need of a man in their life. As long as the majority of Christian women continue to be more interested in being educated and career-minded, they will not have success in dating or the possibility of a long-lasting marriage covenant.
>
> Brian

> Women need to understand that when they turn down offers of help from men in major things such as installing a window air-conditioning unit or in minor things such as carrying their groceries, we feel as though we're being deprived of our "job." Chivalry isn't dead. At least it won't be if women will allow us to be chivalrous.
>
> Matt

At Joshua Harris's 2004 New Attitude Conference for singles, Dr. Al Mohler, president of Southern Baptist Theological Seminary, said:

> The sin [of delaying marriage as a lifestyle option] is shared by women who think they'll put off being a wife and mother until they can establish their professional identity. "I want to do this for myself before I turn to marry." I would beg you to rethink all that.

Is that what the majority of single Christian women think? Do they really decide not to marry and seek careers first? Here's a fictional scene I like to imagine when thinking of criticisms like this: a put-together woman in a business suit marches out of her house with briefcase in hand. Lining the sidewalk are dozens of suitors with flowers and rings at the ready. They each yell: "Marry me! Be my loving, God-honoring wife!" But the woman just walks on by and says, "Sorry, boys, I'm off to work!"

No, this doesn't happen, but you'd think so given some basic misconceptions out there clouding the issues of dating and marriage.

The first is this: "Because there's no definite line between what men and women can do with their lives and because a woman can be self-sustaining, she no longer *needs* a husband." This misconception assumes that because women now have choices, they categorically use them to put their selfish desires for money or respect or power above that of God and the family institution. What such thinking does is equate a woman's heart with her career aspirations, as if they were the same. It also equates traditional labor division with the model of marriage. However, this doesn't add up. The idea of a division of labor in a marriage wasn't prescribed by God or nature—*we* placed that standard on relationships.

In *As for Me and My House*, Walter Wangerin Jr. talks about how, in past eras, families had to work together for survival. In that cooperation, labor would be split into what the group of men would do together and what the group of women would do. But we no longer live in that age. The industrial age and now the electronic age "have taken the basic labor out of the family's hands. The old distinction between 'men's' work and 'women's' work has lost its purpose and force."[6] But still, these cultural habits remain, and some men remember them as the way it's "supposed" to be. That doesn't mean traditional gender roles within a marriage are wrong, but it means we shouldn't make assumptions that "the wife will do this and I will do this" in relationships. As Wangerin writes, true, lifelong marital sharing has nothing to do with gender roles. Instead, what makes a relationship work is sharing gifts, whether in a traditional way or not. How this looks in each marriage will vary and is determined according to the needs of the relationship and the individual gifts that best serve the relationship. And this reality isn't affected by changing cultural trends.

Now, of course, men are called by God to be the spiritual leaders of the home. So in dating, do we steer clear of women who have it all together and can pay their bills and are living full lives? I don't think so. Being a spiritual leader of the home isn't defined by making more money or not being the one who cooks and does laundry. It's also not defined by who first thinks the other is pretty cool and acts on it. What is key to being the spiritual leader of the home is, as a Promise Keepers newsletter once said, "being the one who sets the standard for everyone else to follow. Remember, [in Joshua 24:15] Joshua did not say, 'As for my wife, children, or neighbors.' Rather, he said 'as for me and my household.' He declared he would be the one who set the standard."[7]

A second misconception about single women is this: "Because they have lives of their own, they don't *want* to make room for a husband." Let me introduce you to my friend Jen. She directs the youth group at our church, pioneered our congregation's Honduras outreach, runs adventure travel trips, and teaches scuba. At thirty-eight, she's used her single years to do things she never thought possible, like travel to more countries than McDonald's has, learn daring new things, and grow in her faith. As a result, Jen is more streetwise, adventurous, tough, and handy than I'll ever be. But in quiet times—in between youth group paintball games, camping trips in Alaska, and ministering in Honduras—Jen has often told me how much she longs and prays to be a wife and mom. Did Jen "put off" marriage to build the life she has? Did she decide she wanted to be independent and alone to do these things before marriage? Is she a "lover of self" closed off to men's advances or chivalry so she can be a lone ranger? No.

Jen will admit any day of the week that marrying and beginning a family would stand far above these things as life priorities. But, it hasn't happened. So she's *had* to become self-sustaining and handy. And at the same time, she's chosen to use the opportunity of singleness to make the most of her circumstances and create a satisfying and God-honoring life. I'm sure her future husband would be proud to know she's done so much with her life before meeting him, instead of just sitting around, twiddling her thumbs.

Being twenty-eight and not remembering the world any other way, I think it's an amazing and great thing that women have the opportunities to live true to their hearts and not be held down by assumptions of where a "woman's" place is or what "women's work" is. I know I'd wish this for my future wife and want her to bring her own identity into our life together.

Wangerin ends his chapter on these issues by saying this: "Sharing the work of survival means resisting every temptation toward independence, toward personal liberty, toward 'doing your own thing.'"[8] Instead, he argues, a couple does everything for the good of the relationship. Some guys assume that if a single woman is doing her own thing now, she will continue to do so. But, you know, I'm doing my own thing right now too, and I can't wait to make that change.

I can't help but think the majority of women are in the same boat.

INDEPENDENCE, INTIMIDATION, AND INCOMPETENCE

TODD: What causes some men to keep a grip on these misconceptions and past gender definitions? Besides simple pride and a feeling that we're just not needed anymore, I think it could be a mix of several things. First of all, it can give us an easy explanation for the dating drought: *Well, these women chose career over love.* The reality is pretty ironic. Women haven't remained single because they're too independent; they've had to grow more and more independent because the dating drought has left them single.

Second, if we judge women as a whole, it doesn't hurt as much when individual women reject us. I can just blame it on generalities instead of facing the idea that one particular woman just didn't like me.

I think both of these first two reasons behind the "independent" stereotype are also the culprits behind a male stereotype I find troubling. While guys are calling women too independent, women are calling men passive and weak. I think both generalizations are unfair and are not only remnants of years of gender confusion but also subconscious excuses to explain why we haven't been dating. (We'll talk more about this in the next chapter.)

I believe the third and most common reason women get called too independent is simply because men don't know what to do with this cultural shift. For decades and even now, men have tried to figure out not so much what this means for women but what it means for *us*. I think some guys assume that an average woman's independence isn't about her getting the opportunity to live out her heart's passion but about her beating us, controlling us, or proving she doesn't need us. And if you're operating under that premise, then the changing gender roles do make for a scary and intimidating proposition in dating.

Here are some great thoughts from ChristianSinglesToday.com readers on this:

It's very easy to say, "I can't get along with her because she's too independent." It's much more difficult to say, "I'm uncomfortable with this woman because she makes me feel unneeded and useless."

Most men use this technique to keep free of responsibility. It's not that they can't accept a woman who's able to take care of herself. Rather, the issue is that they can't accept themselves for who they are. They don't want to admit in this modern world that they want a girl who will cling to them and make them feel important.

Of course, there are also women who have issues of their own and overcompensate for their feelings of inadequacy by being too assertive. So we all have problems.

Alan

Sure, independent women can be a little intimidating; it's important for us guys to feel needed and for us to be able to be providers on some level. It's also important for us to have someone we can confide in, someone who can help carry our burdens, someone we can be vulnerable with, someone who can hold us and make us feel safe.

I think a problem is that many men lack the ability to be a provider on a romantic and emotional level, so they rely on being a provider in other areas—financial,

64

```
physical security, etc.—in order to
feel important and needed. Those "other
areas" tend to be, in my opinion, the
areas guys are most intimidated by when
women can handle them without us: career,
leadership, ambition, assertiveness,
and the like. I think many men falsely
interpret "independent" to mean "I don't
need anyone but myself."
```

Jamie

As a guy, I can honestly say I want to feel needed. I don't want to be in a relationship where I can't give anything. It's just the way us guys are built. We want to feel indispensable. We want to be needed. That's the way we feel valued. Someone once told me that a key difference in genders can be seen in their reaction to flowers. Women enjoy them because they *mean* something. Guys have no need for flowers, except for the Venus flytrap. Why? Because it *does* something. Men talk loudest through actions. We often show we love by *doing*, and we know we're loved by seeing our actions appreciated.

So are women typically so independent today that we can't get that sense of feeling needed? Not from my vantage point. Even with my need to provide, I don't look at what I can provide through the lens of traditional gender roles: paychecks, meat to eat, protection from animals. I don't look at strong women like Jen and think, *Well, there's nothing I could provide there!* No, because I know there are a lot of places of need in Jen's life that she'd love to turn over to her husband—not because she has to, but because she wants to.

Besides that, in a home where the man is the spiritual leader and a provider, the marriage is still a give-and-take relationship. Each person has weaknesses where the other provides. It's called partnership, and both members are dependent on each other and their gifts in some way. Maybe she's a stay-at-home mom while I provide the income. Maybe it's the reverse. Or maybe she can't cook but makes more money than me. Whatever it is, I want her to be dependent on me in some way. And maybe dependent isn't the way to put it; maybe instead I should say that I want to be the knight in shining armor. I want to win her. And I want to be integral to her life every day. I want to be able to care for her. And I don't see at all how a woman wouldn't want that just because—by virtue of remaining single into her late twenties or after—she owns a town house, can balance a checkbook, or can shovel her own driveway.

Of course, an overactive sense of self-dependence can be detrimental. I once dated a woman who, by personality type and not because of how long she'd been single, had a hard time letting anyone get too close. She liked being the only one she had to depend on because she then kept herself from being let down by anyone. She may very well have been too independent for a serious relationship.

Other women are uneasy with letting a man open a door for them. Others have bought into the cultural stereotype that men are passive dolts. (Again, we need to get over the generalizations about both genders. So I ask women to just cut us some slack and not jump to the conclusion that men are now all wimpy and weak. While both genders are making sweeping generalizations about the other, nobody is just saying hi to each other.) I think there are also women who may have developed hard hearts—and this happens to men too.

However, I honestly don't see any of this happening on an epidemic scale like the "too independent" critics would claim. Still, I think it's beneficial for women—and men too—to evaluate their life course and prayerfully consider where their heart's desires lay. Are you listening for God's individual call on your life? Are your priorities centered on what God wants? And are you keeping yourself open so that can happen?

In addition, both genders need to consciously work on keeping their hearts and minds open to be what a person of the opposite gender needs. And of course, prayer works wonders in reaching this delicate balance.

Because there are so many misconceptions in the area of gender roles, I really liked what Kevin, a reader of ChristianSinglesToday .com, had to say:

> I would like to believe that the underlying purpose of the old rules of how men and women were to behave around each other was to show women respect. When I open doors or carry things, I intend them to be signs of respect and honor.

Let's be honest. Even in the fifties, women could open doors for themselves. They had opposable thumbs! So, I agree that the things men do for women aren't always a matter of what women need but instead are what we *want* to do for them. And, usually, what *they* want us to do for them. So let's just do it. I'm betting women—no matter how independent we think they are—will be more than happy to let us step in. At the same time, guys, we can embrace all the things women now bring to relationships.

And women, let us help you. I don't suggest you let us do things because you can't do them for yourself. Nor am I asking you to roll over and play dead so we can be manly. But realize we do things like opening doors as a sign of respect and honor—not because we think you're incompetent.

5

Making the First Move

Still Only a Man's Job?

Camerin: A funny thing happened when I asked the readers of my singles column whether or not they think it's OK for a woman to ask a man out on a date. There was a huge gender divide. The women, by and large, communicated that it's perhaps OK but certainly not preferable. Most of the men communicated something along the lines of "Bring it on!" I read these responses with a sinking sense of revelation, thinking, *No wonder we're not dating—both genders are sitting back waiting for the other to make the first move!*

Here's a sampling of typical responses:

```
    I think it's great for a woman to ask
a man out. It helps that man with the
guesswork and/or embarrassment that come
from being rejected by someone who's not
```

interested. With the expanded roles,
responsibilities, and accomplishments of
women, I don't think it's out of place for
her to ask him out on a date.

Michael

I don't think women should ask guys
out. I want to see men take leadership and
initiative not only in dating but in other
areas of life, including leadership roles
in the church. Our culture has methodically
worked on making men look stupid and
ineffective. I'm not proposing we go back
to the male chauvinism of the 1950s, but I
believe God created men to be leaders.

Cindy

One of the overarching issues seems to be what a woman asking out a man represents. Women have made strides of independence in other areas of life, so stepping up to the plate in this arena seems both logical and symbolic in many singles' minds. And for others, a man not being the one to take the initiative in a relationship brings into question whether he can initiate in other arenas of life. Is this a sign that he isn't capable or willing to be an initiator and leader? Such big issues drawn from such a seemingly simple question: "Wanna get some coffee?"

STILL WAITING ON LOCKER BOY

Camerin: The first time I asked a guy out, he never answered. I was in high school, and I asked my current crush to join me for

70

a school dance. OK, so I asked him through a note stuffed in his locker, which I admit is totally lame. But he never answered, leaving me feeling like a complete loser and swearing I'd never ask a guy out again. I didn't exactly make good on that threat. But I admit the few times I've initiated dates since then have mainly been situations in which I've needed a companion for my company's Christmas party or a wedding.

Part of my reluctance in this area is confusion about what exactly it means if I'm taking a role traditionally held by men. How do you know if the guy thinks it's cool or "too independent" for a woman to ask him out? And how do you find out without tipping your hand about your interest? And if you do the asking, does that mean you set the whole plan for the evening? Do you pay? Do you pick him up? Yes, I know it doesn't have to be that complicated. You can always meet for a simple coffeehouse get-together. But these are the issues that swirl through my head when I even contemplate asking a man out.

There's also the issue of what it says about the guy who doesn't initiate. Now, if we're talking about a guy at church or work whom you've spied from afar, the argument that he lacks leadership potential for not approaching you yet doesn't hold much water. The guy's got to know you exist before he can be expected to make any moves! But I admit I wonder about men with whom I've shared some ongoing flirty banter, with whom there seems to be growing chemistry, but from whom there are no invitations.

For example, I once interacted with a guy on an Internet dating service, exchanging several chatty emails about our shared interests, faith, and family backgrounds. When the conversation turned to our common love of movies, I mentioned a wonderful vintage movie theater in our area that I said he just had to visit. I figured this was a great open door for a movie-date and a first step toward a possible in-person meeting. I mean, we were both on a dating site, so we both obviously had interest in getting into a relationship, right? But instead of any invites, he simply said thanks, he'd have to check that out sometime. And the witty emails continued. I scratched my head in confusion . . . and started the mental process of scratching him off my "potential" list.

Sure, I could have asked him out. But, as many men I've talked with about this issue have told me, it's helpful to have some sense of the person's interest before you take the risk of issuing an invite. And yes, I believe in meeting men partway in the arena of date initiation. But my mention of the movie theater—even my presence on this dating site—was my attempt at meeting partway. And I didn't sense him budging to meet me there. It's in these types of situations that I start to wonder what a "failure to initiate" indicates about the guy.

I resonate with the way single-girl Terry reflects on this issue:

> It's so much better when the man makes the move. I know they feel the pangs of uncertainty and risk when they do the asking. But apparently, from what we've learned from sociology, these pangs *motivate* most men. They like the challenge. These pangs *don't* motivate most women. According to research, women evidently get their happiness from being desired, and men get their thrill from the chase.
>
> There's nothing like the thrill of attracting a man. And there's nothing quite so demeaning as having to make the first move because he wasn't attracted enough to do it himself.
>
> Terry

WHAT DOES IT REALLY MEAN?

Camerin: I think the reason why some women see the "failure to initiate" issue as symbolic of a larger problem is that it can seem like another link in the passive chain for men. As we've discussed in previous chapters, men seem to be MIA at church. Many men feel as if we women are "too independent." And now, when there seems to be interest on our part, guys can't pick up the phone or email us to ask us out? When it seems symptomatic of a larger pattern of passivity, it's downright frustrating for women.

But, when I stop and contemplate actually asking my current crush on a date and my palms start to sweat, I begin to understand men's potential hesitancy. And when we women face the other possibilities that the guy we're interested in might have sworn off dating for a while after a painful breakup, or might need some pretty strong clues that we're interested, or might be against dating someone at work or church because of the potential pitfalls, we begin to give guys a bit more grace. And then there's the ultimate possibility no one wants to face—that the guy simply might not be interested in you. In many cases, it's so much easier to call men "too passive" than to face this real and painful possibility— especially if you haven't been in a relationship or even on a date in some time.

I admit I was judgmental of men who didn't initiate dates until I heard two of my married female friends share about how they were the ones who'd initiated the first date with their now-husbands. These are friends I admire with marriages I respect. My friend Michelle had been friends with her now-husband for so long that the leap from friendship to couplehood was a risky undertaking—and one that therefore needed both of their involvement. My friend Ingrid says her husband is so shy that if she hadn't asked him to come fix her malfunctioning phone and then offered to cook him dinner as a thanks, they might never have gotten romantically involved. Neither of these friends' husbands are wimpy or passive or henpecked, as many single women might expect. This is simply how their love stories unfolded.

Another key point to these stories is that obviously these women had many months of dating to observe whether or not their now-husbands had leadership and initiative-taking qualities. This only underscores why it takes time, prayer, keen observation skills, and input from others you respect to figure out the true character of a potential date or mate. And why we must refrain from knee-jerk frustration or fear and take each relationship and person on a case-by-case basis.

LEADERSHIP DOESN'T MEAN BEING RAMBO

 TODD: Of course, a majority of men are going to give a thumbs-up to women asking them out! It's like asking them, "Hey, do you want a free hamburger?" (OK, it's *kinda* like that . . .) But the real question is, What does it say if a woman initiates the relationship?

I've often heard women say that if a guy they're interested in isn't asking them out, then he must be "gutless" or incapable of being the spiritual leader. I don't believe that. Let me tell you a secret: guys aren't mind readers. Just because you like him doesn't mean he has any idea. It also doesn't mean he's actively crushing on you. Sure, we can be a bit oblivious when it comes to romance. (Not only do we need signs, but we sometimes need big blinking neon ones.) So if a woman has an interest, she may have to prayerfully choose whether to let the guy know about it—not because he's too timid or obtuse but because otherwise he just might not real-ize she's interested. And that doesn't mean he's a slouch. (That's only true, I believe, if a man has interest, has prayed about it, and fails to act on his interest. But I don't buy the claims that this is overwhelmingly common.)

Because I know women may have interest in a man who doesn't notice or already have interest in her, I don't think initiation by a woman automatically sets a dangerous leadership precedent. But of course it could. Luckily, it's not a one-shot deal. After a woman does make that move, she can observe the rest of the relationship to see if the guy models godly leadership. We see this in the Bible (Ruth 3). Ruth first approached Boaz and made him aware of her interest, and then he took the lead in the relationship. If Ruth can make her interest known and then let Boaz take things from there, then I think we can reasonably assume this translates to dating today. (And the good news: no one has to sleep in barley!) But this doesn't mean it's the best option. Rich wrote to ChristianSinglesToday.com, saying,

> Today's society has emasculated men to the point we no longer have a clear image of what it means to be a man. Women asking men out leads to us shirking our God-ordained responsibility. And it puts women in a role they don't enjoy. It's not a sin, but I believe it's a lack of discretion and unwise.

Rich is right about one thing: men can live up to the "image of what it means to be a man" by taking the lead in relationships, by pursuing what we want, and by showing some courage. But I don't think men have to be Rambo. Being a leader doesn't mean going out on a limb completely on your own. Instead, I think a healthy relationship, even at the beginning, means a give and take. Both men and women can give signs of interest—finding obvious excuses to email or call, making kind gestures, etc.—to ease into a relationship.

I once noticed that my feelings for a female friend were shifting. As I considered whether I wanted a dating relationship with her, I noticed that for every conversation or email I initiated and every little note or silly little gift I gave her, she answered in kind. It was like one of those dances you see on the Discovery channel of animals showing interest in one another (except without all the prancing and feather shaking). Finally—just as a friend—she invited me to come with her and a couple we knew to a concert. I couldn't go, but I could tell what the greater message was. I asked her out days later, and she said yes.

I've seen emails from women saying that it's hard for them to have interest in someone and then "just wait . . . and wait . . . and wait" for the man. But waiting or doing the asking are *not* the only options.

MEETING IN THE MIDDLE

Camerin: I agree with Todd that there are things women can do besides ask a man out or sit and wait for him to ask us. I think we all can agree it's daunting to ask someone out. There's the potential for rejection that can be humiliating, especially if you have to face that person regularly at church or work. So it stands to reason that a guy would want to be fairly certain of a yes before stepping up to take that risk. Enter the Breezy Email. At least, that's my regular mojo, if I have anything remotely resembling mojo.

For example, many years ago I met a guy at a club a friend and I used to frequent during the swing-dancing craze. He and several of his church friends were regulars, and we always seemed to hit it off when we saw each other there. Somewhere in our conversations he gave me his email address to follow up on another swing-dancing club he told me about. And you bet I found an excuse to send him a quick, chatty email. I made sure to include some sort of question for him to respond to if he felt so inclined. To my delight, he did.

I admit to using the Breezy Email Approach many times since, and usually with positive results. The beauty is that it's a relatively low-stress, low-risk way to communicate "Hey, I'd like to get to know you better." Sure, the guy may never respond, and then it might be awkward the next time you see him. But I still think it's only fair for women to share some of that initial give-and-take leading into any potential dates or relationships—at the very least through means such as an email, asking them to help us fix something in our home, or inviting them to join a casual group outing. And yes, to do the asking if we feel so inclined (and brave!). I don't think it's fair for us to simply sit back and expect men to read our minds and then to take risks we're not so keen on taking ourselves. It seems like the very least we can do is to offer a few hints of our interest.

I also think it's important for us to be open to the invites that do come our way. No, not saying yes to any ol' Joe who asks us to a movie. But I've heard from too many men who say they stopped asking women on dates because they're tired of getting shot down. And I've heard female friends deliberate about whether or not to accept an offer for a date because they weren't immediately sure they wanted the guy as a boyfriend or spouse. Maybe we women need to do a better job of meeting men in the middle not just with our initiation but with our responses to their initiation as well.

DIGGING DEEPER

Camerin: There was another theme to those emails I received about whether or not it's OK for women to ask men on a date that points to a larger, overarching theme of frustration on the part of many singles. Obviously there's a fair amount of past hurt and anger motivating these disparate opinions. Exhibits A and B:

If you ask a wussy guy out and the relationship continues, then don't whine when you end up married to a wussy husband who won't take initiative in your family. This is exactly why there's such an increase in older singles. Guys today appear to be gutless, and it takes far too much hinting to get them to wake up. Basically this is an indication that their masculine character has been watered down. We want MEN back! Not the androgynous creatures created by our godless environment.

Catherine

I think it's a good idea for women to ask men out. Several of us Christian guys have been snubbed by judgmental Christian women who make excuses to not go out for coffee with us. They're basing the decision to turn us down on external features. Also, most Christian women we go out with never return our calls after the first date. That's just rude and cowardly. Due to this, many guys I know have stopped asking Christian women out unless we see a sign from them. It's too hard putting our heart on the line and being vulnerable all the time. I think women should be willing to take risks and ask us out if they claim they want equality.

Randy

From reading such hurt and emotionally charged responses, I get the impression we've gotten to a place in time where asking someone out is akin to jumping off a cliff. There seems to be that much fear, dread, and anticipation of pain involved. And it's as though we're all standing on the cliff's edge, saying back and forth across gender lines, "You go first." "No, *you* go first!" So I suspect some of our confusion over who should ask whom on a date and our finger-pointing across gender lines is actually a smoke screen for the deeper issue of everyone fearing the risk of initiating a relationship.

SO MANY UNKNOWNS

TODD: I agree that initiating a relationship and putting yourself out there is just scary. Sure, the realistic worst-case scenario is that the woman I ask out tells me no, but there's a lot of messiness that makes it worse. In fact, there's so much messiness for Christian singles that this simple invitation to get to know each other better is a big reason why we aren't dating. And yes, men, that falls heavily on us.

Why aren't we asking women out? Obviously the answer is going to vary. In some cases, it's simply a matter of waiting for God's timing. There's also nerves, awkwardness, and all kinds of questions. What if the "signs" I saw were just my imagination? Will asking her out ruin our friendship? Should I even consider it if we work together, go to the same church, or are in the same Bible study?

There's additional pressure because of the biblical standard (Eph. 5:22–32 and 1 Peter 3:1–7) for men to be the spiritual leaders in the home. Of course, I want to live up to this. But in falsely taking that to mean that I must lead and initiate everything from day one of a relationship makes me feel a weird sense of urgency to act. *It's my duty to initiate a relationship*, I think. *I can't be a timid man who won't lead in the home! I've gotta act.* What has this led to? Well, whenever I sense any sort of a connection with a woman, I begin to freak out because I feel like I have to rush into action before I appear weak and she gives up on me.

Certainly some of us *are* initiating relationships when we see open doors. (Perhaps Christian single men are acting on interest, but it's just not obvious because there's so many more Christian women active in our churches than men.) However, when a great number of our Christian sisters—and some brothers too—haven't dated in more than five years, we need to look at whether we, as men, are acting on our interest and opening the God-given doors we're shown.

AN OPEN DOOR . . . OR ANOTHER REJECTION?

 TODD: Many guys have told Camerin and me that they aren't asking women out because of painful pasts. One Christian man wrote me: "In a situation where you, Todd, might pray for a relational door to open, many of us pray that we don't get the door smashed in our faces, since that's what seems to happen every time."

There's a lot of pain out there. The trick is how we respond to it. I've sworn—more than once—I'd never ask a woman out again, due to bitterness and anger. It's easy to rationalize our way out of having to face more pain with excuses and generalizations such as "All women are the same," or "Christian women say they want dates, but I've been turned down twice, so they don't know what they want." With these excuses, it's easy to just throw in the towel and blame the pain on everyone but myself.

After I was turned down one time, I reacted bitterly and told friends that Christian women just weren't interested in dating. Camerin cautioned me about rationalizing. She said, "Don't paint all Christian women with a broad brush." She's right. Sometimes, we can talk about "Christian men" and "Christian women" as if they are a product line that operates a certain way. In fact, not long ago I was interested in a girl but told a friend, "I thought I saw these same signs from others who then rejected me. She's going to do the same thing." But she didn't. What if I'd used my faulty logic as an excuse to not pursue her?

Here's a reality too many of us try to ignore: relationships require some discomfort, pain, and risk. Guaranteed. Asking someone out puts us in a vulnerable position—we're putting ourselves out there for what basically feels like a judgment, an evaluation. It can feel like *American Idol*. We put ourselves out there, sing our little song, and wait for Simon to rip our heart out. After having that happen a couple of times, it makes sense that we'd be gun shy. So we just don't do it. We pull back. We put up walls to protect ourselves. We stop asking, and we use our hurt as a shield to protect us from more pain. The truth is, though, that we're blocking out the good with the bad.

When you think about it, it's logical that rejection is part of the process of finding someone who's a right fit. It is a selection process and a learning journey. And, yes, the good far outweighs the bad. The problem is that along the way, we let those no's carry too much weight. As Christian writer and radio host Dr. Henry Cloud writes in one of his books,

> Don't give a potential date the power to decide for you whether or not you are lovable, likable, or desirable. Get the love and validation that you need from your friends, from your spiritual community, and from God. Develop the security you need, and from that place, go out into the dating arena. . . . Don't allow getting turned down to be anything but a learning experience and evidence that you tried. Remember, dating is not supposed to make your life miserable. Dating is about growing—spiritually, personally, relationally—and having some great experiences. Don't let dating get you down, and don't put too much stock in any one date or any one person.[9]

I agree. Giving up on the other gender or not following the direction you may feel God leading you in because of a fear of rejection is surrendering the desires for romance he's given us, missing out on the good of dating, and possibly turning our backs on what God wants for us. And he does always, in the end, have his best in store for us. But too many of us—men *and* women—often think this means there won't be any pain along the way. In fact, we can slip into thinking we don't have to do any work to get there. I often talk about praying about a dating potential, looking for open doors, and trying to discern how God is leading you in dating, but this is not to say we should sit and wait for a big miracle or sign. Instead, I mean we need to lift our interests to him, try to please him with our dating and try to learn his voice. We often rely on the pleasant and safe notion that God is going to drop Mr./Ms. Sexy/Smart/Funny/Perfect at our doorstep and we won't have to do a thing or risk any pain. Fireworks will ring out. Cartoon birds will sing. *Not only will they just show up*, we think, *but we'll know it's right and won't have to go out on a limb.*

OK, I know I just mocked the idea of a dating option just showing up on our doorsteps, but one night, that's exactly what happened. There was a knock at the door, and I peeked out to find an attractive and charming door-to-door saleswoman. *God is better than Domino's,* I thought. But there were no cartoon birds. We didn't gaze at one another as music swelled in the background. Instead, we chatted for a few minutes, I thought she was intriguing but didn't act on my interest, I bought lots of whatever she was selling, and then she walked away. Was this an open door from God? Did he send her there for me? Well, I don't know, because I didn't act. But I do think this is an illustration of how God works: he does provide open doors, but we have to choose to walk through them. We have to do our part.

DON'T JUST SIT THERE

Camerin: Todd brings up a great point about a trend unique to Christians—the notion that God will drop "the one" on our doorstep at the perfect time and that our only role is to wait for that day. In some ways, for believers, the question of who makes the first move—us or God—overshadows the question of which gender is supposed to initiate a date.

Recently I was chatting with a friend from out of town who told me that in her corner of the country, the singles population is quite sparse. As she shared her realities, she wondered aloud if taking advantage of Internet dating services or personal ads is at all akin to lacking trust in God and his timing. Does the fact that she isn't married yet mean God still has things for her to learn and accomplish in this season? Or does it mean she just hasn't run into the right guy yet and needs to keep her eyes open? Or does the fact that she doesn't often meet new people in the normal course of life lead to the logic that she might have to be a bit proactive about circulating with other singles? What's our role as Christians who believe in a sovereign, all-powerful God but who also live in a fallen, complicated world, and what's God's role?

Some singles compare looking for a mate to searching for a new job. We pray for guidance while simultaneously perusing want ads, circulating resumes, and going on any job interviews we can land, all the while trusting God to open the right door. Others, such as one ChristianSinglesToday.com reader who wrote me a few months ago, give God a much larger role. This reader asserted that if God wants her to be married, that even if she were stranded on a desert island, he'd still bring Mr. Right to her. (Though at that point, I'd hope her priority would be a boat, not a man!)

Of these two options, I lean toward the first. When I look at the Bible and the way God has traditionally worked amidst his people, I see that action is usually required on our part. Joshua and the Israelites had to wade into the Jordan before it would begin to part (Josh. 3:7–17). Several times Jesus commanded people to wash in a river (John 9:1–7) or to rise and pick up their mat (John 5:1–9) before they would be healed. Time and again, God works in our action, meeting us in our steps of faith. Why do we think the arena of dating is any different? Sure, God *can* bring Mr./Ms. Right to our doorstep. And if you feel God telling you to sit back and wait on him in this way, by all means, obey what he's telling you. But for most of us, I think the more accurate question is, *Will* he bring a spouse to our front steps? Is that the way he wants to work in our particular circumstance? Are we boxing him in to only work in one certain way?

Sure, you can take this thinking to the extreme and run ahead of God, making the active pursuit of a date or spouse an obsession or an "idol" in your life. As with so many things in life, prayerful balance is a must.

Personally, I see dangers in sitting back and waiting for God to do all the work. It can lead to a powerless feeling in our singleness, which can make it a very frustrating journey. Yes, there's comfort in knowing God's in charge of our love life. And he is, but leaving all the work to him can make us feel impotent and inactive, and it can lead us to blame God for not meeting our desires if no one happens to show up on our doorstep for years on end. And really, what would that look like? Some guy knocks on my door one day and says, "I'm the one you've been waiting for; God sent me"? I don't know about you, but that would freak me out. More realistically, I have a feeling God nudges us to attend that photography class at the local community college or to join that committee at church—and does so for a single man or woman who's a great match for us. Hopefully we're not so intent on sitting at home waiting for our doorbell to ring to act on that nudge.

WHERE DO WE GO FROM HERE?

 TODD: OK, so what can we be doing as "our part"? Well, I think of three things.

First, let's cut each other some slack and drop the generalizations about the other gender. We guys can try not to view each woman as "the next one who's gonna tear my heart out." If you have an interest that you've prayed about for a while, act on it. And it would be great if women didn't box us in with rules and regulations. Over and over I've heard women say things like "I won't say yes if a guy asks me to go out *sometime* without a specific plan." Not everyone is comfortable with the same things. So, for both genders, it comes down to this: take some prayer-soaked chances, act on interest, treat each other like individuals (and not a vast gender), and give some guy or girl the opportunity to surprise you.

Second, cut yourself some slack too. A friend recently told me about a new dating prospect in her life. However, she was hesitant about it because she didn't know if he was the love of her life. Sometimes I think we can put too much pressure on ourselves before acting on or responding to an interest.

Third, and most important, I think we need to pray not just for open doors but for the wisdom and openness to see them—and the confidence to open them (or at least flirtingly wave through the window).

6

Dating Non-Christians

The Appeal of the Forbidden Fruit

TODD: My friend Steve isn't a Christian, so I was surprised when he introduced me to his new girlfriend: a committed member of my church. *Wait a minute,* I thought. *She's with Steve?*

As their relationship progressed, I felt twinges of jealousy over Amber. It wasn't that I was especially attracted to her. Nor was I singing the eighties pop hit "Jessie's Girl." But I did think it was unfair: *Here I am, a devoted Christian guy, searching for a committed Christian woman . . . and Steve gets one. Here's a woman of God in Steve's arms, and he could care less.*

I was also confused. How could Amber consider marriage with someone who doesn't share her beliefs? *Was* she considering marriage? Could he respect her beliefs on sex and purity? *Or,* I wondered, *is she not keeping to those?*

Amber's relationship with Steve isn't a rarity. The temptation to date non-Christians is very real. And, in a way, it may even be logical with all the confusion and droughts we've talked about. Plus, in daily life, most Christians will come across far more non-Christian dating potentials than devoted Christian ones. And because the non-Christian dating scene tends to be much more open and aggressive, those nonbeliever singles are standing by with invitations to dinner ready. But as logical and tempting as it seems, Camerin learned the dangers of dating a non-Christian.

JAKE, THE NON-CHRISTIAN

Camerin: Some of my first real conversations about the dangers of dating a non-Christian took place in college over Chocolate Chipper Sundaes at Perkins. There, with members of my Bible study, a friend and I quizzed our fellow member Emily about the guy she was spending more and more time with. This guy didn't share her faith. Emily assured us he was a "really great guy" and that we needn't worry since they were "just friends."

Well, three months later these "just friends" were dating. A couple months after that, Emily stopped going to church. And not long after that, her attendance at our study became irregular. If I didn't know the dangers of dating a non-Christian already, Emily's story only underscored how tricky it can be. What was most difficult to understand was how Emily, a strong Christian, could fall for such an obvious, easy-to-avoid temptation.

Eight years later, during a year-and-a-half dating drought, the situation didn't seem quite so simple anymore—especially with Mr. Tall, Cute, and Blue-Eyed asking for my number. It was ironic that I met this guy, Jake, at a church. At a friend's wedding, I spied him in his dark suit and preppy glasses and was internally gleeful when I noticed later that he wasn't wearing a wedding ring. I quickly put together that he was a friend of some friends of mine and was pleased when he sat down next to me at the reception.

Sitting there in the church basement with friends and family, I enjoyed chatting with this funny, talkative, well-dressed man.

So when Jake asked if he could call me sometime, I gave him my telephone number and did a mental dance of joy. The next time I saw Jake was when we met for dinner with mutual friends. Over the meal, the guys swapped fraternity stories about stupid things they'd done while drunk. For some inexplicable reason, Jake still intrigued me. Several days later, Jake asked me to meet him for coffee. As I spent time one-on-one with Jake, I discovered he was easy to talk to, intelligent, devoted to his family—and, as I suspected, a non-Christian.

That realization should have ended my attraction. But I was drawn to this cute charmer who was showing interest in goody-two-shoes me!

In the weeks that followed, Jake and I exchanged flirty emails and occasionally hung out with his friends. When their conversation turned to drinking or their love of going to Hooters, I'd grow silent or roll my eyes and offer a speech about women not being objects—failing to mention, unfortunately, that our value comes from being made in God's image. Jake and his friends were more amused than convinced by my occasional ranting, so the conversations usually gave way to teasing arguments and laughter.

I told myself spending time with Jake and his buddies was harmless fun, maybe even God's answer to my prayer for more non-Christian friends with whom to share my faith. That is, until Jake asked me to join his family and friends for a weekend at a rented beach house. I was caught off guard. Suddenly my relationship with Jake didn't seem casual anymore.

Faced with the decision of whether or not to go, I finally asked a few Christian friends for advice. Maggie, a hopeless romantic, suggested that spending a weekend together would give me the chance to discuss matters of faith. Yet somehow I had the gut feeling the weekend would be more keg party than Kum Ba Yah. Max, my best guy friend, told me to run as fast as I could in the other direction—not just from the invite, but from Jake in general.

I figured I needed more info to make the right decision, and sent a breezy email to Jake asking about the weekend sleeping arrangements and whether or not there would be lots of drinking. He replied that while there might be some drinking, I wouldn't have to be involved. "You'll have a bed to yourself all weekend, and I appreciate your conservative views; it's part of what makes you YOU," he wrote, adding a smiley face next to it. After reading Jake's email, I felt giddy with the excitement of having someone interested in me—and guilty that Jake still didn't know the biggest part of what makes me me: Jesus Christ.

FRIENDS TO THE RESCUE

Camerin: I finally made my decision about the weekend—and Jake—after I had dinner with Kate, a friend from church. As we wolfed down chips and salsa, I filled her in on Jake's invitation to the beach house. Usually one of my biggest cheerleaders, Kate listened quietly to my whole spiel, then paused thoughtfully for a moment. "You know, I'm glad you finally brought up this whole Jake thing," she said. "I've been worried about you for some time." *Really?* Now it was my turn to listen intently.

"What are you doing with this Jake guy? You know he's not a Christian, right? You can say it's casual, but I see your face light up when you talk about him," Kate said, as my face now grew red with the embarrassment of hearing the truth—which I'd previously denied to others and myself. "He's not worth it. He's not worth *you*."

In the silent moments that followed, I finally faced the fact that I'd only been fooling myself. I'd fallen for Jake with each interaction, flirtation, and teasing email. I also realized most of my attraction had been to his attention. I was one of the many affected by the dating drought in Christian circles, and it had been a while since anyone had shown interest in me. Jake's emails, in which he'd openly expressed his attraction to me, had been refreshing. As a woman, I longed to catch someone's eye, to be pursued romantically. And with no Christian guys stepping up to the plate, I, like many other single Christian women, was faced with a dilemma: a non-Christian or nothing.

In fact, I've heard many single Christian women use this as an excuse to date people who don't share their faith. And I've heard others say the church is going to have to address this dilemma for countless single Christian women—that based on the numbers, many women will either remain single for life or will marry non-Christians. "This challenge," a recently married thirtysomething friend of mine said to me once when we were chatting about ratios and limited choices and such, "needs to be acknowledged by churches and Christian leaders, and dissected to determine the lesser of these two undesired outcomes. These are new realities we need to address."

Regardless, I'd known all along what the Bible says about being involved with someone who doesn't follow Jesus. I'd read 2 Corinthians 6:14—"Do not be yoked together with unbelievers"—many times during Bible studies and sermons over the years. And I'd seen a few Christian friends, like my college friend Emily, date non-Christians then suddenly disappear from church. I should have known better than to fall for Jake. And that was the most difficult truth to swallow.

I thanked Kate for her honesty, then asked her to check up on me in the weeks ahead. After dinner I had a long talk with God; I apologized for boosting my self-esteem from the wrong source—a guy instead of him.

I knew Jake needed God more than he needed me. Part of his attraction to me undoubtedly had been an unconscious attraction to Jesus *in* me, and I didn't want to squelch that. I needed to finesse our relationship to keep it "just friends," but I didn't want my first flat-out talk about God to make God seem like some cosmic killjoy.

Thankfully, before calling Jake to tell him I couldn't make the trip, I discovered I had to attend an out-of-state conference the weekend after the beach getaway. I could tell him in all honesty that being out of town two weekends in a row would be too much. When I told him, I could hear the disappointment in his voice. I think he knew I'd consciously chosen friendship over romance at this crossroad in our relationship.

After that phone call, I gently turned down other weekend outings in favor of more casual weeknight coffee breaks. And while I missed the rush of potential romance, I finally felt comfortable telling Jake about all aspects of my life—including the new ministry I was helping to launch at my church and decisions driven by my faith. When Jake's mother grew ill, I let Jake know I was praying for her.

I also asked Kate to keep me accountable to our mutual faith in God, to ask those difficult yet necessary questions about my motives and my heart. I sought to strengthen my security and self-worth by spending more quality time in prayer and Bible study, hopefully making me less susceptible to future temptation.

In a surprise turn of events, Jake moved out of state a few months after I declined his weekend invite. I prayed fervently Jake would meet some strong Christian men in his new location. I hoped he'd be open to other more positive influences away from his drinking buddies. With this distance, our emails grew less frequent, and I've now lost contact with Jake. But every now and then when he comes to mind or I run into our mutual friends, I breathe another prayer that if he hasn't yet, he'll get to know Jesus.

In the end, what Jake and I both needed—and still need—most is God. That's the most important common ground we share—a truth I hope to keep prominent the next time I happen to meet a tall, friendly, non-Christian guy who asks for my number. No matter how cool he seems or how long of a dry spell I'm in.

"BUT THIS **IS** *DIFFERENT!*"

TODD: Nobody consciously thinks, *Boy, I reckon I'm gonna look for a non-Christian to date today.* Instead, the temptation to lower our standards sneaks up on us quietly. And the temptation can be brought on for a variety of reasons. For my friend Amber, for instance, it was watching her best friend and younger sister get married (both to wonderful Christian husbands) and start families. She doubted God's plan for her and began dating more aggressively to hurry up her own trip to the altar. So when Steve asked her out, her attraction to him—and the idea that he could be her husband someday—far outweighed the serious effect of his beliefs on her faith journey.

Temptation to date a non-Christian can take many forms. Maybe she has looser standards for sexual activity than Christian women. Maybe you just really like her. Or maybe you just see no Christian options. If non-Christians are showing interest when Christians either aren't or aren't around, it can be hard to resist. I mean, if you're getting no results in your search, it seems sensible to drop the one stipulation that's narrowing your potential pool, right?

This rationalization is exacerbated by lots of easy excuses that remind me of the secular dating book *He's Just Not That Into You.* The book features letters from women in awful dating relationships using various excuses to explain that their misbehaving boyfriends really *do* care for them. "But my situation is different," they say. And one by one, the authors shoot down the letters, explaining, "Nope, he's just not that into you."

When it comes to dating non-Christians, we also often tell ourselves, "But this is *different!*" For each excuse though, it seems like the Bible has a response, saying, "Nope, that relationship's just not right for you." Some examples of these excuses:

"But we love each other." My friend Dan married a non-Christian several years ago. They love each other very much, but Dan quickly realized many hardships would stem from the fact that his wife will never really understand his faith.

In 2 Corinthians, Paul warns believers by writing, "Do not be yoked together with unbelievers. For what do righteousness and wickedness have in common?" (6:14). Paul doesn't say love can't exist between a believer and a nonbeliever, but what Paul observes is that a believer and a nonbeliever *cannot* ever really understand each other. How can we expect a person who walks with Christ to be understood by someone who doesn't even know him?

Dan knows this too well. Not only will his wife not share in eternal life, but their differences trickle down to practical matters as well. When facing a problem, they can't rely on prayer together. When Dan is busy volunteering at his church, his wife is less than understanding. In addition, many arguments have started over the amount of Dan's annual tithes. She just doesn't understand the most important thing in his life.

"But he respects my faith." A committed Baptist, my high school friend Jessica had heard the "Do not be yoked together with un-believers" verse in 2 Corinthians dozens of times. But when she began dating Dominick, a non-Christian, she told friends it was OK because he believed in a higher power and was very interested in the supernatural. She argued that his interest and respect for people with devout beliefs was good enough to combat 2 Corinthians 6's warnings that they'd have no common ground.

But slowly, Dominick's intimate and intense influence on Jessica began to reshape her long-held convictions. He did believe in *a* god but had no commitment to him. So when I learned they were sleeping together, I was disappointed but not shocked. Paul wrote in 2 Corinthians 7:1 that we need to "purify ourselves from everything that contaminates body and spirit." Letting someone who doesn't hold our convictions and beliefs into the secret places of our heart surely can wear us down and contaminate the good there.

"But it's my chance to witness." My friend Lacey used to talk about her boyfriend Zach as if she had a secret time machine hidden somewhere. She would say, "Once he gets saved, he'll be the perfect husband." She acted as if it were a given.

I didn't really know what to tell Lacey, because I could understand where she was coming from. I once met a non-Christian girl I really liked and quieted my inner warnings by saying, "It will be fine. She'll become a Christian eventually." But was my chief concern really the status of her salvation? No, selfish motivations were at play.

Several years ago, a woman named Zen Lee explained in the *Columbia Standard* why she dated only Christians. "I do not trust myself to desire the right things or to have the right motivations," she wrote. "Maybe 99 percent of the time the motivations behind missionary dating are impure: a need for attention or approval, [sexual desire], desire for companionship, longing to be understood, or a savior-complex. Every Christian should be wary of the secret motivations of the heart."[10]

And even if our motivations were purely about a romantic interest's salvation, missionary dating is a pretty ridiculous strategy. First off, *we* can't save anyone—no matter how hard we work at it. It's God's call whose heart to work in, not ours. Second, the basic premise of missionary dating is purposeful deception. Do we really want to trick or lure somebody to Christ using our love as bait? I hope not.

Worse than the ineffectiveness of missionary dating is that it actually does the opposite: it hurts our own faith. Like Lacey, we can convince ourselves that everything will be OK once the other person changes. But typically, it's we who change.

Women may be especially in danger of this trap. In 2000, syndicated religion columnist Terry Mattingly wrote about a study that looked at trends in living together before marriage. In the *Journal of Family Issues* study, researchers found that "deeply religious men" far less commonly live with a woman before marriage than nonreligious men. However, "deeply religious women" were just as likely to cohabitate as nonreligious women. Why?

"My theory is that women are willing to make sacrifices for their partners, once they have become emotionally attached," said one of the researchers. "They're willing to make compromises to try to hang on to the relationship. Men won't do that. . . . These girls are probably thinking, 'He's not perfect. But I love him and I can help him change.'"[11]

This is exactly why over and over the Bible warns us, above all else, to guard our hearts (Ps. 119:37; Prov. 4:23–25; Prov. 22:5; 1 Cor. 16:13; 2 Tim. 1:14). It's better for me to not even approach a non-Christian than to tease hurtful motivations.

Of course, that's easier said than done. Luckily, we aren't alone. God can do mighty things through prayer. And he can also do mighty things through the people he puts around us. I try to take advantage of those trusted friends and family members by being open with my life so they can lend me truth and accountability. I try to be honest with them. And to ask them to look out for me and keep me in prayer. In fact, I have even given some loved ones specific permission to challenge me and question me about dating decisions.

Most of all, we need to trust God to build our romantic relationships. And we need him not only as the architect but as a day-to-day presence in both members' lives. Great advice comes from Psalm 127:1: "Unless the LORD builds the house, its builders labor in vain."

7

Internet Dating

Using a Mouse to Find a Spouse?

TODD: In 1727, dating changed forever. According to a British dating site, this is the year a lonely spinster named Helen Morrison placed the world's first classified ad to meet a significant other. Her act—meant simply to widen her dating pool and give her new hope—led her mayor to commit her to a lunatic asylum for four weeks.

Yup, Helen, we know how you feel.

Nearly three hundred years have passed since Helen took that giant leap for singles by searching for a new way to meet a potential partner. And even though the scene looks far different now than a small ad in the *Manchester Weekly Journal*, we can still feel a bit nuts as we log on to an Internet dating service.

But it's not crazy to look for dating partners online. It's not desperate. You know what *is* desperate? Our situations sometimes. Maybe your entire church's singles group is made up of you—or you and thirteen people with the same chromosomes. Maybe you haven't met an eligible Christian bachelor or bachelorette since the first *Bachelor*. Or maybe you're waist-deep in intergender friends but don't feel God's call to date any of them.

On top of all that, there's a great irony for single believers. The top three places we may meet new people are the trickiest places to date someone: (1) work, (2) church, and (3) Bible study groups. Everyone has a slightly different take on whether or not you should date someone in these environments. Some churches encourage it, others don't. Some workplaces ban it, others don't. And individuals will all have their own personal stances. Even though I think discreet and mature relationships can do fine with such origins, there is the possibility of upsetting group dynamics, feeling outside pressure from other people, or straining a building romance.

So amidst all the challenges we have, sometimes we have to get creative to find new relationship potentials. We'll hit some of these opportunities in chapter 8. But Camerin and I want to start with perhaps the most defining and revolutionary change to the dating scene in our lifetime: Internet dating. This means allows us to expand our search beyond our congregations and zip codes to bring us new hope. And fortunately, such an effort no longer leads to the asylum.

SURFIN' THE SEA OF LOVE

Camerin: Once upon a time, we all thought singles who looked for love online were foolhardy and desperate. But somewhere along the line, Internet dating became normal. When I sheepishly told people how I met the last guy I dated (I met him online), not one person flinched. In fact, my mother, the woman who used to warn me against talking to strangers, now urges me to sign up for an online dating service like it's eBay or something—like I can just hop online and shop for a hubby. But as any of us who've tried Internet dating will tell you, it's not always that simple.

As I sit here writing, I'm waiting for my heartbeat to return to normal. Moments ago, I sat staring at my phone, whispering aloud to myself, "This is why I hate dating."

You see, over the past several weeks I've been communicating with a guy I was matched with through eHarmony. Based on an hour-long personality assessment, "L" and I were deemed compatible. Soon after, L "requested communication" with me, and we started through eHarmony's many getting-to-know-you hoops of answering multiple-choice and essay-type questions, sharing lists of nonnegotiable qualities in a potential mate, and then emailing one another.

In his last message to me, L suggested we move our communication to the phone. He included his phone number and an offer to call me if I preferred to be the callee. Wanting to hold up my end of the bargain and be a woman of the new millennium, I decided to make the call. But that all seemed so easy and simple and logical . . . yesterday. A few moments ago it dawned on me that though I know all about this guy's job, nieces, and the Bible study he started, I don't know how to pronounce his unusual name!

While in the end the "dating gods" were smiling on me and I got his answering machine, this little drama is a wonderful microcosm of the weird nature of Internet dating. Meeting and getting to know someone through email is simultaneously intimate and anonymous. I can communicate with a guy while in my pj's in the comfort of my own home, pouring out all kinds of personal thoughts, and still not be sure what his voice sounds like, how he carries himself, or if he's an obnoxious laugher. Come to think of it, I also don't know if he is the thirtysomething investment banker he claims he is or really a thirteen-year-old punk.

On the other hand, the Internet has been smashingly successful at bringing together old classmates who have Googled former flames in hopes of giving a relationship one more go. So I know it's a feasible way God can bring people together.

Even when Internet dating doesn't lead to marriage, it still can be fruitful. For me, the biggest bonus of going to the Internet to cast a wider net for dating potential is that it ended my dating drought. I've been in two dating relationships in the past year thanks to the fact that I swallowed my pride and plunked down the cash for an online dating service. Sure, both relationships were short—and they both ultimately ended. But I feel privileged to have met both of these guys. And in the wake of these romantic rendezvous, I've become a bit more confident in my interactions with the opposite sex. It's as if these relationships affirmed that I wasn't unappealing to men, it's just that I wasn't meeting any new men to appeal to. Once I was getting the right "exposure," dating happened. And I suspect that's the main hurdle for many singles who wish they were dating—a lack of new faces in their day-to-day routine.

With this renewed confidence, I've traded desperation for discernment—knowing that the next single guy I meet isn't going to be my One Great Hope for a husband. Also, interacting with men in a romantic light has reaffirmed my femininity in a way I have yet to experience outside male-female interactions. What's interesting is that this affirmation and confidence only seem to attract more opposite-sex attention, which begets more affirmation and confidence, which begets more opposite-sex attention. While many of us have experienced the inverse spiral—dating droughts that lead to shaky confidence and desperation, which lead to scaring off the opposite gender, which leads to even lower self-esteem and more depression—it's nice to know there's a positive pattern to be had if we can just shift the tides.

That's not to say that Internet dating is the great cure-all. I have a couple of friends who tried it for more than a year with no results. Others got burned by dishonest daters or unhealthy attractions. As with most things—such as diets or evangelistic efforts—what works for some won't work for others. Which just means we often have to try many methods before finding the one that works for us. Personally, I'm glad I gave Internet dating a chance.

In this process of looking for love online, I learned some valuable lessons about Internet dating. Mainly that email chemistry doesn't necessarily equal phone chemistry doesn't necessarily equal in-person chemistry. Each time I took one of these steps forward in the communication food chain with an online match, I found we'd taken a bit of a step back in our rapport with one another. Though we'd exchanged many long emails back and forth, the first time we talked on the phone it was initially a bit awkward. Likewise, when we met in person for the first time a couple weeks and many hours of phone chats later, I recall us sitting across from each other in a restaurant booth laughing nervously and saying hesitantly, "So, um . . . hi." Sure, we got our footing fairly quickly in each new realm of communication. But each step was a reminder that no matter how much conversation and closeness we'd shared, there was still some disconnect between the way we'd met and the way we ultimately want to relate with someone in a romantic relationship.

This wasn't my first lesson in the difference between online chemistry and in-person chemistry. Many years ago, I'd used the Breezy Email Approach to initiate conversation with a guy I'd been pining over for months. When I finally found some common ground with him through mutual friends, I zipped him a quick email. I held my breath in anticipation of a response and was elated when he sent me a nice message with telltale questions included (translation: this indicates an interest in further communication). Yippee! For weeks we emailed each other witty messages about life, work, and faith. He's a big fan of top-ten lists, so we started emailing wacky lists of increasing cleverness to each other. I was always excited to see a message from him in my in-box as I knew it would include commentary on my last witticism and new tidbits sure to make me laugh. But, sadly and surprisingly, when we finally got together in person (he asked me out in an instant message), the chemistry was nowhere to be seen. I found that he was still living in the prankster glory of his college years and had a whole crude side to his humor that I couldn't quite relate to. Neither of these things came across in our email correspondence. After a few outings, we just stopped calling and emailing each other. We both knew the moment had passed. And such is the risk of email romance.

Based on these experiences, plus a few other online adventures and those of my friends, here are a few Internet Dating Guidelines I now live by:

Be clear about your faith. On Match.com, singles can list their brand of religion: Hindu, Atheist, Christian, etc. They also can list how often they attend church. I was amazed while perusing Match .com at how many guys listed themselves as Christian (promising!) then answered that they only attend church at Christmas and Easter (bummer!). I've also observed that "Christian" doesn't necessarily mean one who follows the teachings of Jesus, and "spiritual" can mean anything from tree-hugger to one who worships Satan. Even though eHarmony is often thought of as a Christian site, it's certainly not limited to believers. Thankfully you can often tell where potential matches stand spiritually by seeing if faith or Jesus come up anywhere in their personality profile (especially in the questions about who's been most influential in their life, what they're most passionate about, or what five things they can't live without). As for identifying yourself as a believer—no, you don't have to list the entire Apostles' Creed when communicating your beliefs. But it wouldn't hurt to mention that you believe in God *and Jesus* and that your faith is foundational, important, or nonnegotiable in your life. And if you're tempted to broaden your standards to increase your number of potential dates, read chapter 6 again . . . *fast.*

Be vague about your vital stats. We all know how readily available information is on the Internet. So even if you don't list your phone number or address, if you've told someone enough info about you, he or she can find these vital pieces of info through a fairly easy Google search. For example, years ago I "met" a guy online who worked at his family's restaurant. Through Googling the type of restaurant, the city in which he lived, and the guy's first name (oh, don't act shocked, you've Googled people too!), I happened on to the restaurant's website, their entire family story, and the guy's address. Really, I'm not a stalker! However, I did have a friend in that area of the country and wanted to tell her to try out the restaurant—it sounded yummy from his description. I didn't go searching for the guy's home address—but with the press of a few buttons, there it was. Because of that ease of access to important info, I don't list my city, my last name, the name of the company I work for, or my home phone number until I'm sure the guy I'm communicating with is on the up-and-up. We've all heard the occasional news report of people who've been stalked (and sometimes worse) by someone who found them through a personal ad online. Clearly it's better to err on the side of caution.

Listen to your inner cynic. Just because a love interest says she's a twentysomething never-married living in suburbia doesn't necessarily mean she is. On the flip side, and more commonly, beware of what a potential date *isn't* telling you. You're only hearing the details about someone that he/she wants to reveal. If she's a psychopath, is thousands of dollars in debt, has been unemployed (due to laziness) for the past year, or has serious family issues, she's probably not going to announce it right away, if ever. Obviously when dating we usually put our best foot forward in order to impress the other person—whether on an innocent level or to a manipulative degree. But at least in person there are visual clues to tip you off to misinformation or lack of vital details. Through email, we don't have that advantage—a fact worth keeping in perspective when evaluating a date's potential.

Don't wait forever to meet. My experience with Breezy Email Boy shows online chemistry doesn't necessarily translate to in-person chemistry. So to avoid getting enamored with someone through copious amounts of email and then getting your hopes dashed when you eventually meet in person, I always urge newbies to the world of the online love search to get to that in-person stage sooner rather than later. Of course, it's vitally important to use your head and to take *enough* time to make sure your potential love interest is on the up-and-up before agreeing to meet. And always meet in a very public place, and let others know where you'll be. But not belaboring the process and not allowing yourself to get really emotionally attached before an in-person meeting could save you a lot of potential heartache. Yes, that's challenging if the person lives in another state. But I've heard too many stories of people who fell for each other through lengthy, sometimes daily, emails and instant messages—and who sometimes even confessed love for each other—only to have the whole thing fall flat when they finally met in person.

THE NEW LANGUAGE OF LOVE

TODD: It's amazing how much our world has changed in the last one hundred years. Our grandparents' generation must often sit back and think, *How did we ever live without this?* I mean, forget little things like electricity, penicillin, or airline travel, I'm just amazed by computer animation and George Foreman grills.

To me, one of the most amazing changes is in interpersonal communication. How did we ever live without the Internet, email, or cell phones? I once asked a kid in my youth group to call 411 to get a number for me, and it was like I'd asked him to churn butter for supper. He hopped on his laptop (not literally) and had the info in no time. The truth is, technology has completely changed the way we interact with other people (or don't interact

104

with other people, like my computer friend). In the early days of telephones, it must have felt weird to be able to talk to someone and not be face to face. Eventually, you didn't even have to be standing still to talk on the phone—you could do it anywhere! You could also send mail over the Internet in seconds. And now, you don't even have to wait those pesky minutes for someone to write back. You can just IM or send a text message. Soon, we'll just buzz thoughts at each other.

All this ease and convenience in communication has changed not only how we *meet* new dating potentials but also—and most significantly—the day-to-day business of dating. IM makes long-distance dating easier (and cheaper). In email, we craft responses to sound much better than the way we actually talk. And with cell phones, we can reach out and touch our significant other at any time (well, depending on how many free minutes we have left). Just think about all the ways your dating relationship would be different if you were using the communication modes of only twenty years ago!

In fact, communication has evolved to the point that for a wear-my-emotions-on-my-sleeve guy like me, getting to know someone is almost *too* easy. For instance, I met Heather several years ago at a camp we both volunteered at. We had great initial chemistry, and although we lived about sixteen hours from each other, we vowed to continue getting to know each other long distance. In retrospect, I realize Heather and I had little in common other than faith and general likes and dislikes. Had we lived in the same zip code, I think Heather and I would have gone on a second or maybe third date and discovered our chemistry was more about first-meeting flutters than long-term commitment. But because all we had at first was phone and IM communication, we shared lots of personal information, secrets, and parts of our hearts before we were ready. We hadn't had enough face time to evaluate the relationship but instead shared with one another because we could. By the time we saw each other a second time, we'd gotten too emotionally invested for what was really a second date.

It's just so easy to type things and hit send as if you're typing into a void—and not to a real person. To me, email or IM can feel like an electronic diary where I just spill stuff I'd never say in person. After Heather, I learned to watch how much I share in email or IM in order to guard my heart. Now, whenever I'm writing an email that's revealing or intimate in any way, I either keep it for a face-to-face conversation or I save the letter for a bit and go back and read it to make sure I'm not being too candid. Often, I'm surprised by the depth of what I'm about to share.

But this ability to share is of course the greatest benefit of these new modes of communication. Unlike what it would have been for our grandparents, dating isn't hindered because we live in separate towns. In fact, I once actually enjoyed when a local relationship turned long-distance. The two of us were free to concentrate on getting to know each other via email, phone, and IM. Without physical distractions or spending our time small-talking or figuring out where to go to eat, we focused on what made each other tick.

Of course, misjudged chemistry and misunderstandings (even with emoticons ☹!) can be common with techno-dating, but Camerin and I still believe the mix of age-old getting-to-know-you techniques and the new benefits of technology give us a hefty advantage as we meet, date, and fall in love in a new age.

And it's all far more fun than churning butter.

8

Matchmaking

Something Old, Something New, Someone Borrowed, Someone Blue

Camerin: The first time I heard about "speed dating," I dismissed it as a bad by-product of our fast-food, romance-obsessed culture. I mean, what's next, drive-thru dating? "I'd like one tall, dark, and handsome Jesus-follower with a side of sensitivity to go."

But the more I thought about it, the more I realized this could be a great way to avoid some of the downsides of other ways to meet a romantic prospect: those long, drawn-out blind dates and never-ending email interactions from Internet dating services. Given the gender ratio disparity we discussed in chapter 3, the thought of being in a room with twenty-five bachelors, let alone getting to interact with them all one on one, seemed like an answer to my prayers.

For those of you unfamiliar with this new dating phenomenon, let me bring you up to speed. At a typical speed-dating event, each single woman sits at a separate table across from a man. Everyone enjoys a one-on-one mini-date with the person in front of them for three to eight minutes (depending on the host organization's setup). When the buzzer sounds, one of the genders switches tables. After each encounter, participants mark on their scorecard whether they'd be interested in getting to know the other person better. Afterwards, the host organization alerts participants to mutual matches (meaning both people marked yes for each other).

Though I searched relentlessly for a Christian speed-dating event in my geographic area, I found none. Instead I settled for one sponsored by a secular organization, HurryDate, just a stone's throw from a megachurch in my area. Surely some nice Christian boys in the neighborhood would show up!

I invited several single friends, knowing I'd chicken out if left to this adventure on my own. Three brave souls—Todd, Kristee, and Kim—accepted the challenge. And that's how we found ourselves on a random Wednesday night—standing in the doorway of a suburban Chicago restaurant called Fox and Hound, nervously awaiting "the hunt."

A MATCH IN MINUTES?

Camerin: In brief, here's my speed-dating experience by the numbers:

Dollars to join the adventure: 35

Age range of those in attendance: 25–35

Men and women who attended: 17 and 16, respectively

Minutes for each "date": 3

Friends who looked at me like I had three heads when I invited them: 2

Times I changed my clothes before deciding to wear tried-and-true all black: 7

TODD: And here's my quantitative night:

My age at time of event: 26

Women who sardonically asked if I was even old enough to be there: 5

Three-minute dates that felt like 15 minutes: 4

Male attendees who were apparently engineers: 15

Times I changed my clothes before the event: 0 (I'm not sure I even *own* 7 different clothes combinations . . .)

ON YOUR MARK, GET SET, DATE!

Camerin: When Jodi, our hostess for the evening, blew the whistle to start things off, I found myself face to face with Chad, a guy who spoke very fast and blinked a lot. He told me he was a lawyer, asked me not to hold that against him, then bleated out a laugh at his own little legal humor. At the end of our three minutes, I discreetly circled the N next to his assigned number.

My conversation with my next "date," Kurt, about our common love of writing, was just getting good when Jodi blew the whistle again. Definite yes for Kurt. My time dragged on with Nate, a transplant from Texas who missed the wide-open spaces of his home state. Being more of a city gal myself, I marked no.

As the evening progressed, I also was impressed with Dave, a pharmacist working on his doctorate. He was easy to talk to and seemed genuinely impressed when I told him I wrote and published a book. Yes!

My faith in Christ wasn't the easiest topic to bring up in three minutes. For example, when Doug, an editor at an educational book publishing company, asked me which magazine I work for and I replied *Today's Christian Woman*, he paused for a second, then asked, "So, are you like religious?" Oh, brother. "Well, my faith is very important to me," I responded, "but I'm not sure what you mean by 'religious.'" He went on to talk about Bible thumpers and those who try to "cram their beliefs down your throat." Dear me, no.

A LEARNING EXPERIENCE

 TODD: For some reason, I took the speed-dating experience pretty tongue-in-cheek. This isn't to say I wasn't trying, but for various reasons I wasn't clicking with many of the women. Some weren't Christians, others were obviously not enjoying my company, and some just were in a different place in life than I was. And since I was convinced I wouldn't find the love of my life that night, I was able to just have fun with the process. Here are my notes about a few of the women:

"Swears more than Chris Rock."

"Way too many cats."

"Too intense. Really angry."

"Not over last boyfriend."

"Hates men?"

To tell the truth, the best conversation I had on the Night of the Speed Dating—which I capitalize here because it sounds like a cool horror movie—was probably with Jodi, the event organizer. Sure, she was attractive and friendly, but the main reason I enjoyed chatting with her was because she made this night—which I viewed as an experiment anyway—even more educational.

I got chatting with Jodi because every guy had to sit out one round since we outnumbered the women by one. When Jodi sat next to me, I asked her for speed-dating secrets. She said, "The key is to make them remember you. Stand out." As I looked around, I realized some guys already knew this because they were wearing loud, memorable shirts. But Jodi went on to explain that guys who do well at speed dating ask unique questions that open up creative and memorable discussion. She warned against questions like "Have you done this before?" or even "What do you do for a living?" in favor of more imaginative and personable queries like "What was your favorite pet?" "What would you do with a free Saturday?" or "Have you ever killed a man?" OK, Jodi didn't suggest the last one, but I'm sure the woman I posed that question to hasn't forgotten it.

I did end up with one romantic potential after my speed-dating experience, but that prospect ended after one date. So, what I took away from my speed-dating experience were lessons about meeting, chatting with, and getting to know women. As Jodi said, it's about being memorable and unique. To me, that meant not fearing being me. Not holding back from a stupid joke. Not hesitating to ask if they've seen the original Star Wars trilogy or if they associate more with the Cubs or the White Sox (which in Chicago says a lot about a person). And not fearing rejection.

Too many times in dating I try to be who I think a girl would want me to be. But that night, because I felt nothing was at stake and Jodi told me to stand out, I fell back on just letting my true, goofy personality come out. And when I walked out of that place, I honestly believed that if none of the women were interested in me, that was OK—at least I had fun and stayed true to myself.

Talking to sixteen different women back to back also helped show me what attracts me to a woman during a first encounter. (This isn't to say I realized what I'm looking for in a wife—like specific interests or beliefs.) I noticed that the women I gave a "yes" to all shared one thing: the way they reacted to *me* during our three minutes. Basically, they had fun with it too. That's not to say all of them were extroverted and goofy like me, but they were obviously being themselves, were answering naturally, and made the date into a back-and-forth dialogue instead of a Larry King interview. Some of the quickest no's I handed out—besides to Cub fans and the cat lady—were to women who whipped off sterile answers that felt like they were phoning it in: "I'd probably use a free Saturday to relax."

No, I didn't find lifelong love during my sixteen three-minute dates, but I did learn some things to keep in mind when meeting a woman at a party or while on a future first date—no matter how long or short it is.

THE AFTERMATH

Camerin: After the final whistle, Todd and Kristee, with whom I'd carpooled, debriefed with me at a nearby coffee shop. Kristee and I chuckled when we realized Kent, the soccer player, had made sure we both knew he works out "five times a week." We laughed even harder when Todd regaled us with his notes from the evening, such as "Number 13, really fond of frogs, no."

The next morning we all logged onto the HurryDate website and entered our yes's and no's. Twenty-four hours after the event, we were able to view our mutual matches. I received four. When I perused the brief self-profile my matches had created on the site before the event (something we all did), I learned more telling information. I mentally nixed the atheist, as well as the guy who for his ideal match marked "doesn't matter" for everything except age (which skewed young) and body type (which skewed supermodel-thin). One of my matches emailed Kristee and Kim almost identical messages within a day. I never heard from him, and mostly out of wounded pride I didn't email him. That left Dave, the pharmacist working on his doctorate. I crafted a clever message (which took me about six drafts), sent it, then never heard boo from him.

It was interesting to see the way our opinions about speed dating shifted as time went by. Initially, we all agreed it was a fun way to meet new people. Once you've been in the same job and church for a while, meeting new singles is a challenge. One friend pointed out that speed dating can be a nice antidote to the extreme seriousness with which many Christians approach dating. Speed dating, in some ways, is a nice way to break that tension and to get singles loosened up and interacting again.

But as time went by, our positive reactions faded. It was easy to feel boosted or deflated based on the number of matches we received. That only reinforces society's idea that self-esteem comes from romantic love instead of from the truth that we're valuable because we're fearfully and wonderfully made by God. And my initial excitement at being in a room with a bunch of bachelors eventually was replaced by a reminder that it's quality, not quantity, I need. Good single men may seem scarce, but in reality, I only need one God-approved guy.

Overall, my friends and I learned that while you can speed up dating, you can't hurry love.

COMMON GROUND

TODD: While I had fun at the speed-dating event, I felt like it wasn't worth the time, money, or emotional energy I put into it because of my commitment to marry a believer. I decided if I ever did speed date again, it would have to be at a Christian event. Not only would it be fun, exciting, and adventurous to rotate through a room of Christian women, but I also would be assured of some common ground.

When you meet someone by chance—at the grocery store, coffee shop, or tractor pull (just seeing if you're paying attention)—there's a lot of guesswork. Of course, happy Christian couples meet in these seemingly random ways every day, but the more obvious places to find common ground are at church singles groups, Bible studies, etc. But like Camerin said, when you've been swimming in the same dating pool for a while, the scenery starts looking awfully familiar. I think there are two big ways to introduce new faces into your life:

Shake up the circles you're in. I'm not saying just up and move to a new church or let finding a spouse completely dictate your life. But, if you're down because you're in a drought, check out a Bible study at another church. Go on a mission trip. Volunteer with a local organization. Join an inter-church sports league. Honestly, even if you don't meet Mr. or Ms. Right, you're at least having new experiences and meeting new people.

Be open to the friend setup. When you're meeting the friend of a friend or even going on a blind date, you know there's some common ground: hopefully in your faith and definitely in the type of people you hang out with. It's still a risk and can be tricky, but meeting friends of friends can be a true blessing.

One night several years ago, my best female friend, Jodi, and I were spending the day hanging out in Milwaukee. On our way home to Chicago, she suggested we stop by the college of her best high school friend, Ivy. I'd heard about Ivy for almost four years in sentences such as "You and Ivy would be so perfect for each other!" I knew exactly why Jodi wanted to stop by, and I knew Ivy knew it too. As we drove, we saw some fireworks and pulled over to watch. As I sat there quietly watching the display, I prayed about the decision of whether or not to go meet Ivy. I realized I was at a crossroad and that God was nudging me to go. I made the decision to try it out. Ivy and I ended up dating for over a year. No, it didn't work out in the end, but I know God used Ivy to teach me a lot about relationships and about him.

We won't always have to make a conscious decision about whether or not to be open to a friend's setup suggestion. Sometimes opportunities are presented in far more subtle ways. We can miss an opportunity simply because a friend senses we're closed off to such ideas. What can we do? I think it comes down to praying that God will put us in the mind-set he needs us to be in.

THE ART OF THE SETUP

Camerin: While speed dating may be among the newest ways to try to find lasting love, on the other end of the spectrum there's the tried-and-true setup. It could be argued that setups are as old as the arranged marriage, or even as old as Adam and Eve (I mean, there wasn't a lot of choice about that union—though I certainly wouldn't mind having God as my yenta!).

While setups come with the test of time, they also come with a lot of baggage. Who among us hasn't been set up with someone with whom we have only three things in common: we're single, we're Christian, we're breathing. My own story of far-fetched love was when my hopeless romantic friend Charlotte set me up with a guy who lived out of state in a tiny town, managed a fast-food restaurant, loved dirt biking, and was a bit rough around the edges. When we talked on the phone (yes, I agreed to at least talk with him), I could tell he had a good heart and was sold out for God. Admirable traits, yes. Enough to build a till-death-do-us-part, no. Sure, the prospect of a lifetime of free fries held a certain allure, but being more of a citified, indoorsy gal, I had a feeling this romance was doomed from the get-go.

On the flip side, a short while later, a woman I taught aerobics with kept hinting (with the subtlety of an anvil, I might add) that her best friend's son would be perfect for me. Not sure of this woman's spiritual condition, I didn't know how to ask if he was a practicing believer. So I put her off the first 103 times she mentioned the guy. For some reason, when time 104 rolled around, I finally relented—for a casual lunch. Nothing more, and no promises. Lo and behold, when he picked me up at work for our quick lunch date, he had his radio tuned to a Christian station. Hmmm. Nice. Over lunch I discovered that this handsome guy was a newish believer who dearly loved his family and his job as a policeman (mmm!). At the end of our hour together, he asked if we could get together again sometime. I said yes, and a six-month dating relationship was born. While it didn't work out between us in the end, I was glad to have met this great guy. And I never would have met him if I hadn't agreed to the setup.

MATCHMAKING MUSTS

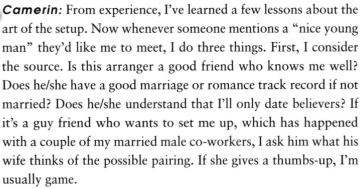

Camerin: From experience, I've learned a few lessons about the art of the setup. Now whenever someone mentions a "nice young man" they'd like me to meet, I do three things. First, I consider the source. Is this arranger a good friend who knows me well? Does he/she have a good marriage or romance track record if not married? Does he/she understand that I'll only date believers? If it's a guy friend who wants to set me up, which has happened with a couple of my married male co-workers, I ask him what his wife thinks of the possible pairing. If she gives a thumbs-up, I'm usually game.

Second, I ask this yenta wannabe why she thinks the guy in question would be a good match for me. If a stumped silence falls over the room, I'm outta there. But if my friend mentions traits that the two of us share, I'm much more inclined to give it a go. This question helps avoid the whole "Hey, you two are both single and breathing!" phenomenon.

Third, I keep it simple. Once I agree to meet the guy, I keep the date short and sweet. A lunch date, as with my former cop beau. A double date at an arcade, like I did with a guy my friends Tim and Michelle set me up with. Showing up at the same party, like I did with a guy a former mentor wanted me to meet. Seeing him interact with others and being able to converse in a nonthreatening group setting helped me eyeball this guy for myself.

Two more thoughts about setups: I've toyed with asking some of my friends to set me up with anyone they think would be a good fit. We all know it's hard to meet new people when you're settled in a routine church-work-community pattern with a closed set of people. And statistics show that a majority of married couples met through their friends. So it stands to reason that many of us are just a few degrees of separation from a great date. Yes, that would mean swallowing some pride and taking a bit of a risk to invite such a setup. But I have a feeling many people around us know someone who might be great for us but they just haven't put two and two together, or they're afraid that we wouldn't go for it, or, worse yet, they think we'd be offended if they mentioned it. Bringing it up first gives them permission to play matchmaker. Which could be a really good thing. Or at least give us some very amusing stories to regale our friends with later!

The other thought is that we singles need to keep each other in mind for potential romantic interests. If a guy doesn't work for me but I have a friend who might be a much better fit, I need to be mature enough to mention it to the two of them. A new trend has taken this a step further by creating parties based around bringing exes (or friends) to share. The events are aptly named "Recycle Michael" parties! But neat name or not, this is tricky. Setting up someone who was interested in you and who just didn't seem quite right takes delicate timing and finessing. But hey, we singles need to stick together . . . and sometimes that might mean sticking each other together.

 9

TV Dating

Reality Bites

Camerin: Sure, *now* I roll my eyes whenever a commercial for *The Bachelor* or one of its serialized cousins flashes on my TV screen. But I have to admit that when the franchise first dawned—with twenty-five single women vying for the affection of Alex—I was intrigued for three main reasons. One, I could relate, because the ratio of women to men felt about right compared to my church singles group experiences. Two, the show felt like a vicarious peek into how the other (non-Christian) half dates. The interactions seemed like what I envision the bar scene to be—overt flirtation, cattiness among the women, strappy little outfits, and more hair flips than on your average cheerleading team. And finally, since I was at the time a casualty of the Christian dating drought, *The Bachelor* at least reminded me that dating hadn't become extinct.

In some ways, the show seemed like telling evidence that the growing singles population in our country was having a hard time finding lasting love. Suddenly TV dating shows, launched back in the 1960s with *The Dating Game*, were focused on *marriage*. And people were signing up in droves to risk rejection on national television in order to seek a spouse (or, admittedly, their fifteen minutes of fame).

But as the show progressed over the following weeks, so did my unease. Was the path to lasting love really paved with so many ball gowns and pajama dates? If these hot-tubbing hotties were being rejected, what chance did I have? Was marriage really a prize to be awarded to the "winner"? Is dating really a competitive sport? As the first season came to a close, I wondered less about what these shows reveal about our culture and more about how much they're affecting it. What messages is this new breed of reality TV slipping into our subconscious?

COMMITMENT SHOMMITMENT

TODD: It's my favorite moment of any reality show: just minutes remain in the episode, and someone is getting booted. Whether it's because the tribe has spoken, they were left without a rose, or they couldn't eat goat intestines fast enough, a contestant has to go home. And I love watching people's reactions to the rejection. When it comes to dating shows, these reactions range from "I'm in love! How can I ever go on without him/her?" to "You didn't deserve this anyway. You don't know what you're missing!" However, I think the most interesting reaction is what I call the "second place at a track meet" reaction.

The best example is Charlie on the first season of *The Bachelorette*. Making it all the way to the final two, Charlie spent a great deal of time with Trista. They seemingly built a strong connection, but when Trista picked Ryan, Charlie didn't talk about how much he cared for Trista. He didn't say he'd miss having her in his life. Instead, he talked like he was stuck with a track meet's lousy red ribbon. It was more like watching *American Idol*. Charlie's grief wasn't from love lost, it was from not winning.

Because of the very nature of dating shows (i.e., a contest), finding a spouse is about competition, attraction, and chemistry—not commitment. Of course, chemistry and attraction are a part of love, but I've learned from personal experience and from watching friends meet and marry their spouses that lasting love isn't built by butterflies and physical attraction. The most important part of establishing a lifelong relationship (besides seeking God's will) is developing a functioning partnership and making a commitment to the necessary time, work, and pain.

On reality TV as a whole, the concept of commitment is underrepresented. Dating is more about sex, fun, comfort, and the thrill of the moment. It's about feeling good. How many couples break up on the *Real World* so that the person living in the house can "be free, experiment, and take full advantage of this experience"? After a while, love feels like a jacket you can just take off when convenient.

You'd assume at first that marriage-based shows like *The Bachelor* and *The Bachelorette* would be all about commitment. But, something about the process is broken. Of the first five seasons of *The Bachelor*, all of the relationships ended soon after the show did. Why? Obviously, part of the blame goes to the medium itself: reality TV just isn't real. *The Bachelor* courtship is like no dating process I've experienced. First, there are twenty-six people involved, not two. Second, dates occur in fantastic venues like hot-air balloons on the French Riviera instead of a movie theater in Kankakee, Illinois. And most notably, the show's structure and TV cameras ensure that no one is being him or herself. You aren't seeing your potential spouse flopped on the couch after a bad day at work. You aren't living day-to-day life in all its glory and struggles. When the couple heads into real reality, the relationship is going to be different.

All of these factors stack the odds against a reality TV couple. But I think there may be something else going on. I worry that it serves as evidence of the mistakes we can make when choosing our spouses.

I know I've had to be vigilant in my own life to carefully weigh what my interest in a woman is based on. *Is it her looks? Am I just interested in having a girlfriend and not specifically her? Am I only feeling those happy, early relationship flutters?* If I had to choose a mate from a roomful of twenty-five women, I think there'd be many temptations clouding my decision. It's easy to get caught up in selfish motivations and not be drawn to the kind of qualities that help establish a healthy, committed relationship.

I think the "Charlie factor"—thinking of relationships as a challenge to win—hurts commitment too. Once we "catch" someone, it's far too easy to just stop there. We can look at it as "Job accomplished. I got her." But that's just the beginning of a commitment that takes daily work, prayer, and attention.

Luckily, most of us aren't being filmed as we date. But even better, we aren't making the decision alone—we have wise Christian friends and an all-knowing God to turn to for guidance. It can be hard to trust and follow God's leading. I'm notorious for not listening closely enough to him because I don't always want to hear what he's saying. So, I'd like to challenge us in three ways: (1) to carefully weigh and pray over why we're interested in a potential date, (2) to not get caught up in "winning" a spouse, and (3) to first and foremost let God speak to us about our romantic relationships.

LOVE AND MARRIAGE

Camerin: Bachelor Bob, from season four, earned the nickname Mr. Kissy-face due to his constant making out with the women on the show. While he later claimed he wasn't that amorous and that it was merely the editing that made it look like he locked lips on every single date, the fact remains that on these shows, the Bachelor or Bachelorette is romancing multiple people at the same time. Sometimes even during the same date! Barring a few singles with questionable ethics, I don't know of many people who would allow the person they're dating to simultaneously make out with others. And where else do you see four guys and one woman on a date? Behaviors people wouldn't dream of putting up with in real life are suddenly OK since there's a TV camera involved. While I don't think this is going to prompt singles to suddenly start dating en masse and kissing at random, I do wonder at how these shows are affecting our perception of love and marriage.

On shows such as *The Bachelor*, *ElimiDATE*, and *Blind Date*, love is something you earn by being the prettiest, perkiest, best-looking in a bikini, smuttiest, least psychotic, or most scintillating conversationalist. Contestants perform, and attention and affection are doled out based on how well they do. Obviously this flies in the face of the sacrificial, unconditional love we're called to by Christ. This biblical, countercultural love is hard enough to keep in focus and to emulate in our own relationships without these televised, in-your-face models to the contrary.

I also marvel at people who claim to be in love after spending a few way-staged dates accompanied by countless cameramen and crew. The first night of the Bachelor Bob series of *The Bachelor*, one of the booted women started crying over how devastated she was to miss out on Bob's love. This was after only one night—one party attended by twenty-five beauties and Bob. Unless they got some major off-camera one-on-one time we didn't see, she was basing this affection for Bob on group conversations and from observations from when Bob was on a previous *Bachelorette* show. Based on that little interaction, she was devastated to miss out on a relationship with him? While I suspect they liquored everyone up to heighten the emotions and drama, this seems to highlight another temptation of these shows—and of the rest of us living our love life off camera: being in love with the concept of being in love.

I think we women are especially susceptible to this temptation. From the time we're little girls, we're shown fairy-tale stories of Princess Love and Prince Charming Romance. Love is the thing. It makes the world go round, and it makes us real and complete. Not lasting love, mind you. That initial rush of new love, the process of falling in love—*that's* the panacea for all the world's ills. That's what every little girl dreams of and every "bigger" girl awaits with starry eyes. Unfortunately, that kind of dreamy new love doesn't last. It either gives way to much less exciting but much more mature and gratifying lasting love . . . or it burns out. And that part of the story, because it doesn't make for good TV or movie fodder, is seldom told. Lasting love, as Todd pointed out, is based on commitment . . . as well as forgiveness, perseverance, grace, and huge amounts of prayer. How many people have only seen these models of new love and have bailed when they get past this stage and suddenly the relationship takes work? How many relationships have been deserted as one or both of the partners have left in search of another new-love high? And how many of these reality shows, with their ball gowns and fantasy dates and their spotlight on the process of *finding* love, have fed this warped view of love and marriage?

SEX-TREME DATING

 TODD: In many ways, dating for Christians looks substantially different than what we see on *Blind Date*, *5th Wheel*, or *ElimiDATE*. One of the most obvious ways is in sexual behavior. On the now-canceled *Meet My Folks*, the parents of a single gal would invariably hook potential dates up to a lie detector and ask, "Do you intend to sleep with my daughter?" No contestant ever said no without the lie detector going crazy.

That's why I so badly wanted on the show. How shocked would a dad be when I—without any beeping of the lie detector—said, "Not unless we get married, sir!" It would be fantastic TV history (well, at least to me).

Even though I hold firmly to my commitment to sexual purity, I have to admit that the sexual content of reality dating shows has affected me (we'll delve more into the issue of sexual temptation in chapter 10). Sure, sexual content is all over TV, but this is supposed to be *real*, so these shows make me think I'm even more of a freak to be holding to my standards. It's bad to become desensitized to casual sex and to start feeling like the last American virgin male. But it's worse when this proliferation gets me thinking, *Boy, what good times am I missing out on?*

I remember one episode of *Ex-treme Dating* when a woman discovered her date had slept with 106 women. I should have been mortified and sad, but instead—as she went home with him to become lucky number 107—I was a bit jealous. OK, I know this kind of activity isn't just immoral, it's gross. And no, I can't imagine and wouldn't want a life like that. But in a very shallow way, I admired his confidence, sexual experience, and allure. Yeah, I still knew it was wrong, and I didn't go out looking to score. But seeing sexual immorality so normalized—and even *desired* by a woman—can lead to two dangerous things: (1) A temptation to give in a bit physically in relationships. *Maybe this isn't so bad*, I can think. Before I know it, these messages have helped my sexual desires go too far. (2) Lustful fantasies that take my mind to places I don't want it to go. For a long time, shows like *Ex-treme Dating* and *Blind Date* were my biggest guilty pleasures. I didn't want to admit it then, but I know now they gave me sexual images and storylines that ate away at my defenses against lust.

Fortunately, Mr. 107 put me over the edge on these shows. I can honestly say that was the last episode of either *Ex-treme Dating* or *Blind Date* I've watched. I had to cut myself off, not because I thought it would change my behavior, but because the sexual scenarios and subconscious messages *were* changing my thoughts.

THE MISS REALITY TV PAGEANT

Camerin: One of the first things that struck me about that first season of *The Bachelor* was how beautiful everyone was. There was nary a pudgy, pimpled, or plain gal to be found. One by one, the women each emerged from their respective limos—their dresses and shoes strappy, their hairstyles straight out of a fashion magazine. Occasionally the television audience would hear Alex, the Bachelor, comment on how hot he thought certain women were. Obviously those women had the best chance of being awarded a rose at the end of the evening and proceeding to the next round.

This first-episode procedure became standard *Bachelor* fare. As did frequent trips to the hot tub. And you can bet that each of the contestants had a bikini-worthy bod. The swimsuit competition, if you will. When you think about it, the show's not really that different from the Miss America pageant. The gowns, the swimsuits, the "interviews" about their opinions of the world. Just instead of the winner earning a crown and the title Miss America, she gets a ring and the title Mrs. What's-His-Name.

Unfortunately, along with the similarities to the pageant come the same objections about the way women are portrayed on these shows. I conducted a round-table discussion on these dating- and marriage-oriented reality shows a couple years ago, and the most fascinating part of the discussion was on this very topic. Here, listen in:

> *Camerin:* As a whole, how are women portrayed on these shows?

Margaret: As objects. In fact, they treat *themselves* as objects. For example, on the first episode of the most recent *Bachelor* series, the producers who chose who would be on the show talked briefly about the women's intelligence, but they mostly focused on the fact that these women had to have bikini-worthy bodies. Based on previous shows in this series, this should have come as no surprise. The contestants knew that's what they signed up for. These shows totally objectify women and tell us that what's valuable about us is our appearance and our sexuality.

Carla: It seems the women on these shows see their bodies as a means to an end—which in this case is a relationship. Instead of celebrating their sexuality as something good in itself and in the healthy context of marriage, they seem to see it as a way to get what they want.

LaTonya: This is an interesting study in postfeminism. On one hand, these women value their femininity and they're working it. They're in red ball gowns and they've got the fluffy hair. But they're using these things as currency in this dating exchange. So I'm not sure if this is empowerment—or victimization.

Lisa: I think it's both. In her book *The Beauty Myth*, feminist author Naomi Wolf asserts that when you see women gaining power in the culture, there's always a beauty backlash that communicates, "No, *this* is what you're valued for." And so shows such as these play into that. Actually, pretty much all our entertainment media plays into that.

What's remarkable to me is that these are intelligent, professional women. And yet they're succumbing to the voices in our culture that say, "No matter what you achieve elsewhere, you're only valuable and lovable if you're sexy and beautiful."

Camerin: But as Christian women, we know that's not the source of our worth.

127

Carla: I think that's a huge struggle for us—how do we feel attractive without compromising ourselves and our values? I wrestle with that a lot. Just how much effort should I put into looking good when I know that's not the most important thing? How much time is it OK to spend doing my hair and putting on makeup in the morning? At the same time, I don't want to look slovenly.

Margaret: Christian women may know their value isn't found in outward appearance, but we still live in a culture that places a high value on that. I'm a psychologist, and one of my clients recently told me, "I know you say beauty isn't what's important. I know my faith says it's not what's important. But *everything* else around me says that's important." Even though we know we should resist, it's difficult not to get pulled into our society's thinking. It's also tough when we feel the negative effects of deciding to be more modest and more concerned with the state of our soul than with the way we look.

Sure, we see beautiful people on TV all the time. And the pigeon-holing of women as sex objects is nothing new. But never before with the word *reality* attached and within the context of such a public peek into the private process of trying to find lasting love. This only seems to take the message "pretty equals valuable" one step further to add that only beautiful, sexy women deserve marriage. And in a singles scene where we're already constantly asked why we're not married yet, this can be so dangerous. It can tempt us to buy the untruth that the answer to that elusive question lies somewhere in the image that stares back at us from the mirror.

And it can also become tempting to try to sex up our image a bit in order to help us lure a spouse. Sure, attraction is an important part of the overall equation of finding a lifetime love. And completely letting our appearance go wouldn't help us any in the quest to attract potential dates. But I fear these reality shows up the ante for what we consider normal and attractive—both in ourselves and in others—and also place a too-high priority on physical appearance and attraction.

WHAT WOULD A *CHRISTIAN* BACHELOR LOOK LIKE?

TODD: So obviously, reality dating doesn't reflect Christian dating reality. But could these differences be reconciled to produce a *Christian* Bachelor? What would that look like? I think this is an interesting notion for each of us to contemplate. Would you stand out as any different if you were the Bachelor or Bachelorette? What if you were a contestant? How would your actions set you apart? What would challenge you?

But we probably won't have to worry about it because *Christian Bachelor* might not make for exciting TV—especially with all those scenes of silent prayer.

10

Sexual Temptation

True Love Waits . . . for What?

Camerin: Christians have a lot to say about sexual temptation. This is all well and good and as it should be. Unfortunately, most of these messages seem to be aimed at sixteen-year-olds. After you get past youth group or campus fellowship, though, the warnings and advice taper off. And if you're reading this, you've no doubt already figured out that sexual temptation at sixteen is very different than sexual temptation at twenty-seven or thirty-three or forty-five.

In some ways, sexual temptation is a bigger issue at older ages. Instead of ending a date on our parents' porch, where there's at least the threat of watching eyes, often we're saying good night in a solo home—or spending the entire date there watching a movie on the couch with nary an accountable eye in sight. We've had more years marinating in our sex-saturated culture, more years discovering there's a lot of gray area between a simple peck on the lips and sexual intercourse. As one of my more frank friends put

131

it, "Being still single at this age means lots of years of foreplay!" Those who have experienced an active sex life, either in a previous marriage, before they became a Christian, or in a moment (or prolonged season) of weakness, find abstaining in this current stage of life all the more difficult.

And with these grown-up realities, the platitudes that are often addressed to the youth-group set about sexual purity seem woefully lacking. Lauren Winner articulates this well in her 2005 release *Real Sex: The Naked Truth about Chastity*:

> I have, by now, read countless books and heard countless lectures on singleness, chastity, and refraining from premarital sex. Many of these lectures and books seem out of touch with reality. They seem naïve. They seem designed for people who get married right out of college. They seem theologically vacuous. Above all, they seem dishonest. They seem dishonest because they make chastity sound easy. They make it sound instantly, constantly rewarding. They make it sound sweet and obvious. . . . Too often the church, rather than giving unmarried Christians useful tools and thick theologies to help us live chastely, instead tosses off a few bromides—"True love waits" is not that compelling when you're 29 and have been waiting, and wonder what, really, you're waiting for.[12]

Todd and I realize we're not going to tackle all the complexities surrounding sexual temptation for grown-ups in one chapter. But we'd like to at least get some honest, real conversations started.

IT'S ALL IN YOUR HEAD

Camerin: If you gathered ten typical Christians in a room and asked them what they think is the biggest struggle for their single sisters and brothers, I bet a majority of them would mention sexual temptation.

It's a good guess. But it's wrong. When we posed this question to the readers at ChristianSinglesToday.com, sexual temptation ranked third (with 15 percent of the vote), behind "loneliness" (32 percent) and "trying to be content in my current life stage" (24 percent). While Todd argues that sexual temptation would have garnered higher numbers if we'd polled only the male readers, I still think the overall breakdown of these responses goes back to the issue we identified at the outset of the book: Christian singles aren't dating a whole lot. Let's face it, it's difficult to be tempted sexually when you haven't been on a date in a couple years!

But of course being tempted to go too far physically in a relationship isn't the only form of sexual temptation. In an entertainment culture full of sexual ethics and practices contrary to our beliefs, the most consistent and alluring battleground for sexual temptation isn't the bedroom but our brains.

I'm startled every now and then when watching *Friends* reruns or *Alias* or the latest blockbuster flick to find myself not at all fazed when a couple winds up in bed together on the first date, or when I find myself even rooting for the consummation of a long-awaited romance or the breakup of a marriage so a third party can enter the scene. I'm not proud of these things, but they're true. And I know from a few candid conversations with friends that there are many of us desperately trying to keep from being products of our oversexualized culture. So how do we do that?

If you think I'm going to suggest tossing your TV or watching only PAX programming and reading only the Left Behind series, you're wrong (unless you feel called by God to do so). Not only would that lead to a narrow intake of artistic stimuli, it would make us somewhat irrelevant to peers outside the Christian subculture. One of the more effective and well-attended outreaches my church staged was a film festival, in which we showed some strategically selected movies and then discussed the spiritual and ethical themes therein.

But on the other hand, there have been times when I've opted out of a movie outing, quit reading a novel, or decided to stop watching certain TV shows altogether, such as *Desperate Housewives* or *Will and Grace*, because, though popular and often well-written, they had me laughing at or rooting for things that are quite contrary to my beliefs. And, let's be honest here, as single people, when we get aroused by certain scenes in movies or in books, there's not much that's healthy we can do with those feelings. Sometimes I'm even more concerned about the subtle ways "reality" dating shows, romantic comedies, and the new genre of "chick lit" can shape our expectations for the opposite sex and romantic relationships.

There are times I feel a bit prudish by deeming certain shows a no-go for myself or drawing other lines. But when I remember that God's just as concerned about our thoughts and motives as our actions (Matt. 5:21–22, 27–28), I know this is the right thing to do. And when I'm spared that niggling feeling of guilt when finishing a novel or walking out of a movie theater, I experience a refreshing peace of mind.

This whole topic seems to be just another reason our relationship with God needs to be daily and active, and why we need to allow him into the messier parts of our lives. I need his guidance to know how to make these seemingly minor decisions that help form my paradigm about major issues. God knows my weaknesses and areas in which I'm especially susceptible and can help me make wise choices that will protect me from unhealthy thoughts or actions. And I know these "little" decisions in regard to sexual temptation that I face between dating relationships will affect the way I handle it in person the next time I'm kissing a guy good night after a "hot date."

This temptation is also a reason we need to allow others who share our faith into the messier parts of our lives as well. I need the loving accountability of friends who will call me on certain decisions when I'm perhaps tuning out God's voice or having a difficult time hearing it. What a vital role we can play in each other's lives, drawing us closer to each other and to God, as we take the risk to be real with one another.

THE GRAY AREA

TODD: If I ever see Christy and Will again, I owe them an apology. I'd also tell them they were right.

Christy and Will are devout Christian friends of one of my ex-girlfriends, Lauren. We'd often double date with them, and we liked them a lot. But in secret, Lauren and I laughed at the way Christy and Will lived out their relationship. We thought they were quaint.

Will and Christy believed very strongly in guarding their relationship against sexual temptation. They wouldn't spend extended amounts of time alone—and never at night. They hugged frequently, shared short public kisses, and held hands, but cut off physical interaction there. Lauren and I, both Christians, couldn't understand it. We labeled them as naïve and silly. I thought, *How can they get to know each other and figure out if they're compatible without* any *physical intimacy? They'll get a real surprise on their honeymoon.*

I was very immature in my faith during my relationship with Lauren. Brought up in the church, I loved the Lord and tried to live my life to honor him, but I was missing something. I wasn't carrying my devotion to him into my day-to-day living. This was most evident in my beliefs about sex. I always maintained a commitment to remain a virgin until marriage because I knew this is what God calls believers to do, but I didn't understand why (1 Thess. 4:3–7). I looked at it as something God just said not to do and not as his loving efforts to save us from the harms of premarital sex. I didn't connect it with preserving a pure body (1 Cor. 6:13) and mind focused on him (Prov. 4:25–27).

This thinking was harmful. By assuming God cautions solely against intercourse itself, I left open a great big gray area of sexual intimacy. I never even thought about where I should stop before sex. In fact, I used to give speeches to my non-Christian guy friends about why I didn't want to have sex before marriage. I'd say, "Guys, I just don't need sex because there's plenty of fun stuff you can do before getting to that!"

Somewhere deep down, I knew all along my attitude was flawed and hurtful. I now realize God was trying to speak to me. I often felt uneasy about the physical nature of my relationship with Lauren, but my sexual desires tempted me on and on. In fact, my criticism of Will and Christy may have been rooted in jealousy—they had guarded themselves when I hadn't, and I knew which way was better.

But my relationship with Lauren didn't change. It was easy to quiet my reservations by telling myself, *What we're doing isn't the same as sex. And it's not leading us to it. It's just growing and sharing with her. Besides, I'm in control and it's not like I'll just accidentally trip into having sex. I know how far is too far.*

A DOWNWARD SPIRAL

TODD: In retrospect, I feel like God used the juxtaposition of my relationship with Lauren and that of Christy and Will to show me an important difference. The trajectory of the two relationships was a real-life case study on why God asks us to keep our hearts pure, focused on him, and closed to sexual temptation.

Will and Christy gradually and steadily grew in their love for each other—both emotionally and spiritually—and they eventually got married. Lauren and I, however, only grew closer physically. It got to the point where physical interaction became our only bond. We grew distant and fought often. Soon, our physical relationship lost all intimate meaning and descended into mere selfish gratification. One night, Lauren said something that shocked me: "I think we're ready to start having sex."

When I think of that moment now, it plays in my head like a movie flashback with an ironic voice-over. I hear my confident voice repeating those words I often told myself, *It's not leading us to sex. I'm in control. I know how far is too far.*

I hadn't guarded myself with a pure heart and had slid down the slippery slope of sexual temptation, even when I said I wouldn't. And while the biggest culprit in my slide was the reckless intimacy I shared with Lauren, Camerin was right when she said our thought lives really determine how we act when physical temptation comes around. I rarely checked my sexual thoughts. In fact, I at times relished them. But yet, I always laughed at the notion that I'd lose control. And now here I was: face-to-face with a woman who was ready to have intercourse. In fact, what scared me the most was that this was the furthest I'd ever felt from Lauren. Our relationship was battered and bruised. I was afraid we'd have to break up soon. But yet, this was when we were most tempted to share the ultimate expression of love. It showed me how God's gift of intimacy can be distorted and misused.

After I told her I wouldn't have sex with her, Lauren and I had some very hard conversations. We broke up soon after. But the most difficult conversations were with God. I had slid away from him and now had to come back, acknowledging he was right all along. This started with me releasing my guilt, sin, and desires over to him. Then I had to learn how to live my life and relationships to really glorify him and to guard my heart. To do that, I've drawn firm physical boundaries.

Of course, that's the million-dollar question in Christendom: how far is too far? I had to look at a few things in order to answer that question for myself. First, I had to honestly look at my specific weaknesses. What excites me to the point that I lose control of my thoughts? What physical activities do I remember not as opportunities to share and grow but because they were titillating? At what point does my physical interaction in a relationship become less about showing my affection and more about what's in it for Todd?

Second, I wanted to make sure I was honest with myself about my weaknesses, so I looked for accountability. I shared my thoughts with a Christian friend and started to gauge where couples I respected drew the line. Would I want my future wife doing this right now with another man? Would I want to tell her I did this in a previous relationship? Would I feel comfortable telling my pastor or youth group kids where I draw the line? And most importantly, I prayed for guidance and wisdom.

It feels ridiculous, in a sex-saturated culture, to be an almost thirty-year-old man doing less in a relationship than many high schoolers. I feel like a freak when I see dating portrayed on TV. And I must sound like a big nerd when friends learn that holding hands with a girlfriend is a big thrill for me and making out is as far as I'll now go. But I'm convinced this is where I need to be to stay healthy in my relationship with Christ. It's funny for me to think that this is the same focus Christy and Will had all those years ago—and I questioned and criticized them for it. I used to think they were naïve and silly, but I now see they were wise and brave.

THE MILLION-DOLLAR QUESTION

Camerin: It was one of the most awkward kisses of our dating relationship—but also one of the most endearing and memorable. As Andrew leaned in to kiss my forehead as we said good night at the restaurant we'd met at for dinner, we kind of ran into each other. I'd erroneously thought he was going in for a hug.

While anyone watching us may have thought this a cheesy, bumbling way to say good night, I knew this innocent peck on my forehead symbolized Andrew's desire to respect me and establish some boundaries.

Over the dinner we'd just shared, he'd brought up the fact that our few-dates-old relationship had progressed to kissing. While he confessed this was quite enjoyable, he also confessed this opened a whole can of worms. Before we got too far down the road of physical interaction, he wanted to discuss our boundaries. Where did we want to draw the line? What were our respective weaknesses that we needed to steer clear of? How far was going to be too far for us?

As awkward as this conversation was to have over burgers—we grew conspicuously silent every time the waitress came by to refill our drinks—I was thrilled Andrew had broached this topic. In fact, it was one of the most attractive things he'd ever said or done in our many hours-long phone chats and handful of dates.

As important as the DTR is for many dating couples, I think the far more important conversation is often the DOB chat: Determine Our Boundaries. Why? Because I think the mother-of-all-dating questions—how far is too far?—doesn't have one conclusive, one-size-fits-all answer.

I don't mean that in a relativistic way. Rather, I think we're all wired so differently and have different things that trip us up when it comes to sexual temptation. It's like how some people can have a few alcoholic beverages from time to time and be responsible and fine and healthy, and other people have to avoid the stuff altogether lest they fall into addiction.

For example, I have Christian friends in healthy, godly marriages who hail from far-flung ends of the how-far-is-too-far spectrum. One friend of mine confided that she's glad she and her now-husband of a dozen years did "a bit of naked stuff" before they wed because it made the transition to sex after marriage a bit smoother for them. I witnessed another friend of mine's first kiss with his bride—during their wedding ceremony. This friend had become a Christian later in life, and therefore had a "past" and needed to draw very stringent boundaries in order to make it to the altar with his sexual purity intact.

Personally, I've found the conversation about physical boundaries to be essential in dating relationships. I need to know if kissing a guy's neck or French kissing really trips a guy's trigger—so I can respect him and not tempt him by doing these things. And I need guys to know my areas of weakness. I've also told some guys, "Here's where I want to draw the line. I need you to hear this and know this now, because in the heat of the moment, I'm not always going to act in a manner that communicates this to you. I need us to work to keep this boundary together." As a woman, I have a lot of appreciation and respect for guys who will work with me on the boundary issue and not just "leave it to the woman" to draw the line of how far is too far, as have been the traditional gender roles in generations past.

Of course, having a successful conversation of this sort requires honesty with ourselves—about where we typically flounder and fail in the area of sexual temptation. I love the guidelines Todd shared about setting his personal physical boundaries. The questions he asked himself are helpful in realizing our parameters—which we then need to share with our dating partner, within appropriate reason, of course. Getting into too much detail about this topic can be tempting in and of itself—and can lead to a certain closeness that, I've discovered the hard way, can then lead to an ironic and impassioned make-out session. This is why it's often wise to have such a conversation in a public location, as Andrew and I did.

And it probably goes without saying that the most important person to include in this conversation is God, who knows how we're wired, who desires our sexual purity even more than we do, and who created us with lips and hands and hormones and therefore knows the best context and limitations for each.

PUT BLINDERS ON ME

TODD: Of course, once you ask yourself all those "weakness" questions and have that DOB talk, the real challenge begins: maintaining those well-intentioned boundaries. After dating Lauren, I reset my physical perimeters and then promptly pushed the limits in my very next dating relationship. Within one night of a first kiss, I plowed right into the territory of extremely passionate kissing. That's right, in twenty-four hours of physical intimacy with a new girlfriend, I was at the limit of what I wanted to do before marriage.

But once again, God moved me past the misstep and used it to teach me and reset my focus on him. I also learned I can't just set a boundary of where to stop. Instead, I need to pace my relationships so I don't get to that line within a week of dating . . . or a matter of hours.

While it's a hard battle to resist temptation when I have a flesh-and-blood woman sitting next to me on the couch, the more consistent and frequent battle, like Camerin wrote, is in my own head. This is why I think that the poll of singles that Camerin mentioned was misleading when it said sexual temptation is the third hardest aspect of singleness. Sexual temptation is a persistent struggle—with or without anyone else around. The media barrage of images, messages, and expectations intensify my consistent and natural urges and temptations. Also harmful in this mix are the ghosts of past experiences. Although the Lord graciously forgave me of my past, those images and feelings still present temptations. With my very humble struggles, I don't envy Christians who wrestle with past memories of intercourse.

A song called "Deathtrap Daisy" by Christian hardcore band Staple captures the battle against our thoughts: "So in love with the memories of you that I have fallen away. . . . So alive in the memories of you that I have died today. . . . I'm so free without you, yet so aware that I am hanging by a thread of grace and nothing more. Sweet Jesus have mercy when she knocks on my door. . . . I'm breaking for my heart to find innocence I've left behind. God Almighty, Giver of Peace, grant me the strength I seek."[13]

Not only do those lyrics touch on the shame, weakness, and power of lust, they point so vulnerably at the answer: Jesus, who extended the grace that erases those past actions (Eph. 2:3–5). And, while I used to roll my eyes at such a "naïve" idea, I've actually found great security in fighting temptation—whether from memories, relationships, or pornographic images—solely in the Lord's strength (Heb. 2:18).

The first step is recognizing that temptation is constant. I can't stop it. Alluring images or ideas can be found anywhere—or they'll just pop up in my head. But the key is that we can stop these thoughts or images from becoming sin. As Martin Luther said, "I can't stop the birds from flying over my head, but I can stop them from nesting in my hair."

By myself, though, I can only stop the nesting for so long. I'm just too weak. But God is strong. I have to allow and trust God to protect me. A friend told me once that when tempted by sexual images or thoughts, he would pray for God to take the feeling away. In fact, he'd ask God to put blinders on him so he wouldn't even *see* alluring images or *think* sexual thoughts.

It's amazing what God does when we trust him and ask him to remove lust from our lives because we can't do it ourselves. I often pray, "Lord, I alone am way too weak to turn away from these thoughts or to resist renting this movie. If I have it my way, I'm gonna look at *Maxim* magazine or think about that woman in a not-so-godly way. But I need you to put a bubble of protection around me. Don't let those thoughts in." I've been amazed by the resulting protection. The Lord has dramatically transformed me. Of course, there are often times I don't pray about my temptations or I pray and then don't let God work. To be honest, it's an everyday battle.

DOING THE RIGHT THING

Camerin: When I started chatting with Joseph at the Southwest gate at LAX, I noticed he wasn't wearing a wedding ring, was nicely dressed, and appeared to be a few years older than me. Perfect.

We struck up the conversation of two strangers waiting on a delayed flight, and next thing I knew we were boarding the plane and continuing our conversation in side-by-side seats. As the flight finally took off, we talked about world travel, the four languages he speaks, my job in magazines, and religion. The latter topic proved interesting as he seemed to be a secular Jew who didn't know much about Christianity. I talked some about grace and the difference between religion and a relationship with Jesus, and he listened with a fascinated, admiring smile.

Though I knew our faith differences made this a no-go for a relationship, throughout our conversation I became increasingly aware of his hands, the shape of his mouth, the stubble on his face. As the minutes turned to hours, I became more and more drawn to him—emotionally, intellectually, physically.

As he leaned back for a nap during the final hour of our flight, I started reading a book, placing my elbow on the armrest between us, which made our arms touch. Neither of us pulled away.

After a few moments, during which I'd reread the same paragraph about four times, he stirred and muttered, "What's happening here? I've never felt such a quick connection to someone. I feel so close to you. Do you feel this?"

Inside my head: *Yes! Yes! Yes!* Out loud a polite, "Yeah, I know what you mean."

"I don't want to sound too forward, but I'd really like to hold your hand," he said.

So there we sat, two people who'd met mere hours earlier, hands entwined, fingers caressing, sparks flying. We talked about getting together for dinner while he was in town. I didn't think I'd found lasting love; I mean, he was a non-Christian who lived half a country away. But I envisioned a nice meal together and possibly a few emails in the future.

In another moment of shared silence, I muttered a wordless, *OK, God, I know this is a bit fast. Help me here if this is off at all.*

Suddenly I found myself saying, "So, you're not like married or anything, are you?" I laughed.

So did he as he said, "Just a little bit."

Whoa.

"Um, *what*?" I stammered, hoping this was some sort of sick humor. "You're joking, right? You're not married, right?"

"No, I *am* married."

I pulled my hand away quickly. "*You're* married. You're *married. You're married*," I repeated aloud as the truth sunk in and the mood shifted completely.

The electricity was gone. In its place a flood of emotions rushed in: embarrassment, disappointment, emotional whiplash, guilt, anger.

We stammered our way somewhat awkwardly through the remaining forty-five minutes of the flight. As I rode the shuttle to long-term parking, slow, hot tears rolled down my face. On the drive home I thanked God for his obvious intervention and poured out all my conflicting emotions.

Over the next two days I was very aware that the guy was still in town, in possession of my business card, and thus my email address and phone number. Part of me wanted him to contact me; the rest of me reviled that part. I knew he wasn't a Christian. I knew he was married. I knew we couldn't have a relationship. But I was still attracted to him and drawn by our unusual, instant click. I know God intervened before I got hurt, but it still was difficult to experience something resembling the kind of instant click with a stranger we all secretly dream about, only to go home crushed hours later. In fact, instead of enjoying more tingles and scintillating conversation over dinner with him two nights later, I showed up for my usual Tuesday night volunteer gig with an English as a Second Language class, where I helped people from Mexico and Eastern Europe with vocab words about the bathroom.

A few lessons became clear with hindsight. As much as some sexual temptation is visible a mile away—you're in a serious dating relationship, you're walking into a steamy R-rated movie—some of it's very sneaky. It wasn't until I was relaying the situation to Todd and he replied, "That guy would've had an affair with you," that I realized the full extent of what I'd walked away from. As Todd wrote earlier in this chapter, maintaining our sexual purity is a daily battle. Sometimes my prayers about this topic have to start from an honest point of weakness: "God help me to *want* to do the right thing (or *not* want to do the wrong thing!)."

My rendezvous on the plane also reminded me that we always need to be on guard and be close enough to God to hear his whispered cautions to us. Also, even though doing the right thing is often much less interesting and fun and can sometimes make us feel a little prudish or geeky in our current culture—it's still the right thing, is still the obedience God requires of us, and is still for our greater good. And some day, my married friends assure me, it will make the joy of experiencing sex the way it was created to be experienced—between husband and wife only—all the sweeter.

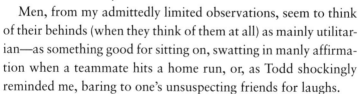

Body Image

The Good, the Bad,
and Those Who Feel Ugly

Camerin: When Todd threatened to moon someone from the backseat of my car (long story), I was struck by the fundamental difference in the way males and females view their backsides.

Men, from my admittedly limited observations, seem to think of their behinds (when they think of them at all) as mainly utilitarian—as something good for sitting on, swatting in manly affirmation when a teammate hits a home run, or, as Todd shockingly reminded me, baring to one's unsuspecting friends for laughs.

Women (and I consider myself an expert here) mostly see their derrières as a necessary evil, as something nearly impossible to clothe appealingly in a pair of jeans or a swimsuit, as something the size of which to obsess over and to ask leading questions about, such as "Does this make my rear look big?" (Note to men: the answer is always no.)

All of this seems to be merely a microcosm of the way men and women view their entire bod. In other words, men seem to view their bodies as a handy place to store their soul, heart, intellect, and the like. Women seem to view their bodies as a reflection of all these things, as something to be judged by strangers and friends alike, and, when we watch enough TV, as things with which to sell organic shampoo and light beer.

It's with utmost familiarity with this female paradigm that I shake my head whenever I receive some of the semi-regular thread of emails from male readers complaining about the overweight single women in their church groups and social circles. "Why don't they take care of themselves?" they wonder. "Don't they know how unattractive this is?" "Where are the trim, godly single women?"

HOW DO YOU DEBATE THAT?

 TODD: "Christian single women don't take care of themselves" seems to me to be one of those ridiculous criticisms, like claiming all Christians are gun-loving, hypocritical, and homosexual-bashing hillbillies. How do you even debate that? I could intelligently debate some claims about Christians, but overweight and unattractive? Come on, what can you even say?

From my personal vantage point of observing Christian single women (and here I also consider myself an expert), I'd say that on a percentage basis, they're just as attractive and just as attentive to their health as anyone. But, I didn't want to just refute one generalization with another generalization, so I did some research to see if there's any correlation between being overweight and any of the three distinctives in question: Christianity, singleness, and being female.

Let's start with Christianity. In 1998, Purdue University sociology professor Kenneth Ferraro found a correlation between being overweight and being religious. His findings applied to all major religions but revealed that Christians on average weigh more than Jews, Muslims, and Buddhists. Of Christians, Baptists tended to weigh the most. "The religious lifestyle has long been considered a healthy one, with its constraints on sexual promiscuity, alcohol, and tobacco use," Ferraro said in a Purdue publication.

> However, overeating may be one sin that pastors and priests regularly overlook. And as such, many firm believers may have not-so-firm bodies. [Also,] overweight people may find comfort in religious settings. Temples, synagogues and churches may provide an important source of acceptance in the midst of a society that highly values fit bodies. In general, obese persons are more likely to be depressed and dissatisfied with their health, but among religious persons, weight had no effect on well-being.[14]

Is there a link between weight and being single? A study conducted between 1999–2002 by the Federal Centers for Disease Control and Prevention found that married people are, overall, healthier than singles. One factor considered was body weight. One statistician involved in the study told the Associated Press that this could be explained by the theory that healthy people tend to most often get married and less healthy people tend to not marry. In fact, a 1996 article in Cornell University's *Human Ecology Forum* reported that "many studies have shown that obese people have more difficulty attracting a marriage partner [and] marry later."[15] One could infer from this that if overweight people are less likely to marry, the result is a greater number of them left in the dating pool.

And then I looked at correlations between gender and weight. According to the National Center for Health Statistics study on U.S. health trends published in 2004, 65.2 percent of Americans over 20 are overweight. This isn't unique to one gender. In fact, the

National Center for Health Statistics reports that 61.7 percent of women and 68.8 percent of men in this country are overweight.

Here's what I find interesting. According to my research, Christians are heavier than the norm and there may be more overweight singles in the dating pool, but neither of these factors has any real bearing on gender—they're seemingly equal across the board. So why aren't more Christian women emailing Camerin to complain about the size of eligible bachelors? The truth is, she rarely receives email arguing this—even though the percentages of overweight men are higher. What's up with that?

I think the answer says more about what Christian men *expect* from Christian women than it actually says *about* Christian women. I'm afraid men are buying into how the media defines beauty. This may mean believing what American culture says a woman *should* look like. I don't think any of us men would say we're looking for a woman with Paris Hilton's measurements, but I suspect we do have a mixed-up perception of what "overweight" or "unhealthy" is.

Human Ecology Forum had an interesting article in 1996 about the changes in cultural attitudes about weight. In it, an anthropologist related a story of watching the Elvis film *Blue Hawaii* with several South Pacific islanders. He says they were baffled as to why Elvis "spent all his time chasing the skinny blonde in the bikini . . . in their eyes, her short, fat friend was a much better catch. This is because in their culture, what we consider overweight is considered beautiful."[16]

In our culture, this is hardly the case. In fact, not only does the majority prefer the skinny girl in the bikini, but also there's an actual stigma against overweight people. This stigma unfortunately affects the dating world—and especially men's perceptions of women. In the same *Human Ecology Forum* article, a sociologist with the U.S. Division of Nutritional Sciences reported the findings of a study on high schoolers' attitudes about dating different body types. He found a high degree of "reluctance to establish a relationship with someone who is fat. . . . The comfort level for studying with, having lunch, seeing a movie, attending a party, and dating steadily, declined for both sexes. Young women, however, were less bothered than young men. More than 80 percent of men said they would not date a very overweight girl."[17]

I'm not innocent in all this. I wrestle with the way I look at women. Often, too much of my attraction is physical. And I've often thought, *If* this *woman's spirit and personality were put in* that *body, would I be interested?* Sadly, I think sometimes the answer may be yes. In those times, all I can do is pray about what I'm really looking for and that my testosterone doesn't run the ship. And I also know that in our age of media saturation, all of us are affected by the messages we get about what's sexy, regardless of gender.

Obviously weight is an important factor in most men's level of attraction (and, to a somewhat lesser extent, for women's as well). And because most of us seem uncomfortable with dating overweight people, it makes sense that there would eventually be more of these people still single. It's sad that this is a reality at all. It is even sadder that this would be the reality for Christians—male or female—because we're adherents to a religion that preaches looking at what people have to offer on the inside. Sure, a person's weight and the way they take care of themselves can reveal something about their personality and character, but we need to consider that in tandem with everything else we observe about them. If we're basing our opinions about attractiveness exclusively on the shape of a person's body, something is off. That indicates we may have a mixed-up perception of what unconditional love is. Or maybe, we've slipped into thinking God will provide us with a spouse who has what *we* value and not what he values. After all, our standards of what is "attractive" or "overweight" are ours, not his.

Of course, I know physical attraction is important to finding a spouse—for both genders. So I'm not arguing that people should completely disregard physical appearance—we are all (and maybe guys a little more) wired to be attracted by what we see. But honestly, I don't think our visual nature is solely the problem when it comes to comments like, "Christian single women don't take care of themselves." Part of the issue is cultural standards, and I wonder if defense mechanisms don't play a part too. After all, it's a lot easier to explain why we aren't dating if we can say, "But there's nobody around me who's attractive!"

After looking through all that research on physical attraction and the obesity statistics, I feel challenged to better care for my own body—not because it will lure me a spouse but because it's an act of worship to our Creator who fearfully and wonderfully made us. Yes, our worth comes from more than physical appearance, but greater worth comes from following the Lord's desires for us to be good stewards of all he gave us. I also feel challenged to pray to let God determine what I find attractive.

WHY IT IS SO HARD

Camerin: I'll admit, there are days when I want to tell those "why don't Christian women take care of themselves?" guys what to do with their questions. But, in an attempt at fairness and understanding, I'd like to hazard an explanation as to why weight issues are so difficult, sensitive, and complicated for women.

There are so many ironies operating when it comes to the messages our society sends about women's bodies that I can't come close to mentioning them all here. Size-two models star in commercials for bacon double cheeseburgers, and actresses with access to personal trainers, hours a day to work out, and personal chefs are portrayed as normal. *People* magazine's annual "50 Most Beautiful People" issue sports scantily clad women opposite men in suits or long-sleeved shirts and jeans (no low-riders here). The average female model is 98 percent thinner than the average American woman, and even then their images are airbrushed and lengthened to make them look even taller and thinner.

We women look at all these unattainable images and unrealistic expectations and eventually want to give up and eat a plateful of brownies in frustrated defiance. Admittedly, sometimes we do. And in the cruelest of all ironies, the extra weight all of this can pack on apparently drives some available men away, making single women that much more lonely and depressed and prone to find solace in Ben and Jerry, thus creating a maddening, no-win cycle.

Yes, we're certainly supposed to take good care of our bodies, especially since the Bible calls them "the temple of the Holy Spirit" (1 Cor. 6:19) and tells us to "present [our] bodies as living sacrifices, holy and pleasing to God" (Rom. 12:1). But it also tells us what's really attractive, such as a life full of the fruits of the spirit: love, joy, peace, patience, kindness, goodness, faithfulness, gentleness, and self-control (Gal. 5:22–23). It also tells us to think about things that are true (Phil. 4:8) as opposed to those that are airbrushed, implanted, or portrayed by a body double. And it's probably a fair assumption that we're told "man looks at the outward appearance, but the LORD looks at the heart" (1 Sam.16:7) because God would love for us to follow his example.

I admit that in our culture, this isn't always easy. Men in the media are often portrayed with exceptionally attractive faces and bulging biceps. And there certainly are single women who've allowed those unrealistic images to affect their expectations when it comes to romance and dating, causing normal guys to feel stuck in a similar no-win situation. In fact, eating disorders and body-image issues are on the rise for men. I think we singles are especially susceptible to the unhealthy body images these dynamics can create because we have no spouses offering words or physical contact to affirm us just as we are (though certainly not all spouses are good at this).

I hope that we, as Christians—both male and female—are adopting the kind of paradigm that recognizes beauty in all its shapes and forms. And I hope this will run through my head the next time I meet a great single guy who has a little extra padding on him or who doesn't have the physique or smoldering eyes that are lauded as attractive at every turn.

Now, if he suggests mooning someone from my car, I'd give a definite "no thanks!" Humor, like body image, must be a Mars/Venus thing too.

NOT JUST A MARS/VENUS THING

TODD: In my first dating relationship, Jackie and I were annoyingly cute and lovey-dovey. One afternoon, we were sitting in my car, sharing a nice moment of just gazing into one another's eyes. And then, she said it: "Why do you have to be so ugly?"

She later played it off as a joke and said I was taking her comment too personally. But it struck deep. You see—besides the fact that guys will moon people on command—body-image issues are not for women only. Sure, we guys will use our bodies for humor. And yeah, we won't often admit it (in fact, if anyone ever asks me about having body-image issues, I'll not only deny I ever admitted this here, but I'll also pretend to not speak English). However, I doubt there are many guys—good looking or not—who haven't at some point privately had appearance issues. But I think men wrestle with our images in a different way than women do.

From talking to female friends over the years, I've discovered that the fundamental issues women have about their bodies boil down to: "Is there something wrong with me?" or "Can I still be desired if I don't look like a Victoria's Secret model?" For guys, body image can affect our self-esteem, but we don't internalize it as much. We don't take negative comments about our bodies to mean there's something wrong with who we are as people. Nor do we worry so much about what we think is wrong. Instead, the question that matters is: "How am I perceived?" When I've heard other men talk about themselves, it's almost like their hang-ups are dents on their pickup truck. Sure, it looks horrible and drives you nuts, but it's just something you hope others won't notice. And you'll try to fix it eventually.

When I was at my heaviest point a few years ago, I knew I was overweight. But it didn't really affect how I thought of myself, except in dark times of self-frustration. Instead, I was just concerned about how others saw me. For instance, I went to the doctor one day, and a young, attractive nurse weighed me. She slid the weights on the scale to a starting point of 150 and started moving it up. I knew I was actually in the neighborhood of 250. And man, was I proud that she thought I looked lighter than I was! To me, this completely validated that everything was fine with my weight—others' perception of me wasn't hurt!

What did finally drive me to a Weight Watcher's meeting more than two years later? A homeless man on the street hoping for change kept yelling at me, "Hey, big guy! Big guy!" That's when I knew I was being perceived as overweight. When I look back at things that have most plagued me in terms of body image, it all comes back to others' perceptions. That's why Jackie's comments that day hurt so deeply: a person I cared for so much perceived me as ugly.

I have a friend, Ken, who had a hard time getting up the nerve to ask a certain girl out. Because of the negative way he mistakenly thought women perceived him, he was shy about approaching this girl. One night, he and I were chatting with some female friends. All three were in relationships, so they very innocently commented that they thought Ken was cute. This insight into how he was perceived by others was apparently enough for Ken. He asked out the girl the next day.

It's funny how affirmation that we're OK can mean so much coming from three random women, when we should know all the time that's exactly what God thinks.

PRESSURE **FROM THE INSIDE**

Camerin: As if the body-image pressures put on us by others aren't enough, there are those that we—especially we women—put on ourselves.

I admit, when I recently ran into an ex-boyfriend at a Friday-night concert, one of the first thoughts that ran through my mind was *Why, oh why did I eat that doughnut this morning at work?* Did the state of my heart or soul, or even my career or finances, breeze through my mind in that oh-so-human reaction of wanting to impress this guy I'd once dated? Oh no, it was the size of my thighs. While I was secretly pleased I'd worn the more hip of my two winter jackets and was having a good hair day, I also silently berated myself for not working out more lately. As the commercial says, image is everything. Sadly, sometimes even in our heads.

Now that I'm into my thirties, this body-image stream of consciousness has reached a fevered pitch. Now I also bemoan my lagging metabolism, my growing population of gray hairs, the new little lines around my eyes. There are times I want to get married yesterday simply because I want my spouse to see me naked before my body goes any farther south—literally. I think about Proverbs 5:18, which says, "May you rejoice in the wife of your youth," and think, *Well, yeah, it's easy to delight in her because she's still young and firm.* I *want* to be delighted in, and wonder if that will be possible when a man has to watch me apply Suede #13 to my hair every six weeks and night cream to my eyes every evening.

I desperately desire a man who'll look past all my "packaging" and anti-aging products and see my heart, my soul, my intellect, my passions, my dreams. But, I realize in moments of clarity, how can I expect a man to look beneath the surface if *my* focus often is only skin deep? If I obsess about the size of my backside, I discredit God, who says I'm fearfully and wonderfully made (Ps. 139:14). If I go to the extreme and base my confidence on my kicky new hairdo or trim waistline, I'm not giving enough value to my redeemed soul.

Perhaps the most difficult introspective question is whether or not we're spending as much time contemplating and prettying up our insides as we are our outsides. In our extreme-makeover, image-is-everything culture, it's tough to keep the right perspective about our bodies. It's tough to remember that, as Christians, we're not just skin and bones, cellulite or rock-hard abs, baby-got-back or buns of steel. We're the dwelling place of the Holy Spirit. We are, all of us, no matter our shape or size, created in the image of our Maker. Perhaps it's when we walk in that truth and confidence that we'll truly be attractive. And perhaps we have to see that in ourselves before we can expect anyone else to recognize or admire our true appeal.

WHAT'S SEXY NOW

Camerin: Last Saturday I had brunch with a friend of mine. As we waited in the lobby for our table, I noticed that we were surrounded by several married couples and their seemingly countless children. Those in the four-foot-and-under category had the rest of us seriously outnumbered. As I cracked a few jokes about fearing a toddler uprising, I noticed that the nice-looking man waiting nearby had overheard us and was chuckling.

The three of us exchanged polite small talk until a three-year-old blonde girl came running up to him and dove into his arms. After a few moments of nuzzling in Daddy's arms, the little girl began wrapping her long pink winter scarf around his head. She was very deliberate in styling the accessory just so, and her dad was a great sport, chatting all the while and appreciating her efforts.

As I watched the sweet daddy-daughter moment, I became disturbed that the more ridiculous the man looked, the more attractive he became to me. It was just so incredibly endearing that this businessman-looking guy wasn't flinching an inch as his daughter used him quite publicly as a mannequin for her latest dress-up game.

This is just the latest scenario I've noticed in a strange pattern signaling a shift in what I find attractive. It all started a couple of years ago when I watched a guy I was somewhat interested in baking in his kitchen during a party he and his roommates were hosting. When I asked what he was making and he replied, "Fluffy white frosting" (for the cake he'd already made), I was sold. I found it oddly attractive that this engineer had quirky specialties in the kitchen. Jerry Maguire may have had Renee Zellweger's character at "hello," but this guy and his trusty mixer had me at "fluff."

This makes me think of the cover line I see on a lot of magazines today: "What's Sexy Now." Inside there are pages chock-full of all the shoes, haircuts, hobbies, and actors the editors deem attractive at that moment. I have a feeling if I looked back at what I've deemed "sexy" over the years, I'd notice a marked shift from eye candy to character issues. Sure, I still enjoy seeing Matt Damon or George Clooney in a romantic flick, but give me a kindhearted man who'll happily schlep my groceries and keep me laughing for years to come to go home with after that movie any day.

It's not as though I was looking for a shallow man with rugged good looks in my younger days; it's just that the older I get, the more I realize what's really important. Seeing how marriages have almost become disposable and being someone who wants a life-long mate, I've had to rethink what I'm looking for in a potential husband. Temporary pleasures—excitement, good looks, lots of money—aren't exactly the kind of things you build a forever on.

So, I'm learning to look a little deeper, to appreciate someone who loves his daughter enough to let her make him look a bit ridiculous in public or who knows how to fend for himself—even in the kitchen. Someone who'll keep me guessing, and growing, and laughing—now that's the man for me. Part of me is glad I've stayed single long enough to realize that abs of steel and a well-defined chest are way overrated, and that the condition of the heart lying beneath is what's really sexy—or not. I'm beginning to suspect that Mr. Wonderful won't be found at a party or trendy coffee shop but at my church's nursery, where he's happily volunteered to play with the kids—and to serve God. Now *that's* attractive.

WITH HIS EYES

TODD: About four years ago, my girlfriend at the time asked me, "You really think you're physically unattractive, don't you? Well, you really aren't."

That helpful, albeit difficult, conversation started a process in which Anne helped me realize that the way I thought others were seeing me was indeed not the truth. She helped me admit I wasn't ugly. But then a month later, we broke up because she told me she wasn't attracted to me. In my mind, that negated everything she'd said previously about my looks. Everything.

This illustrates the biggest way in which my image issues affect my relationships. Whenever I face rejection, I regularly jump to the conclusion that it's about my looks. When my girlfriend said she wasn't attracted to me, I didn't for an instant consider that attraction is more than physical appearance. I took it solely as "I don't find you attractive" or "You are not attractive" and not "I'm not feeling a romantic connection" or "You're not my type."

This is a common trap, I think. I've heard several men say women pay too much attention to a guy's appearance. Their justification for saying this? "Whenever I ask any woman out, she won't give me the time of day because I'm not Brad Pitt!" Others tell tales of meeting women through Internet dating services and not getting any dates. Almost categorically, they attribute this to the fact that they're bald or overweight or "not Brad Pitt." Is this really what women want?

I don't know, actually. Maybe female expectations of their mates have been shifted just as much by the media as ours have. I think women do very much want a man who's attractive to them. But when I see the number of very attractive women out there walking in the mall and holding hands with very not-Brad-Pitt-looking guys (and rarely the reverse), I have to admit that women on the whole are probably less visually oriented than we are. So, I think this complaint can often just be an excuse we use when we're faced with rejection. Maybe it's just easier to blame the other gender for being so close-minded. Or maybe, because perception means so much to us, we just assume that the things we're already nervous about—like our weight, receding hairline, or height—is what turns the women away.

Preventing these attacks to our confidence starts with finding true contentment with ourselves. For me, this process began with changing some things I could change, such as my weight, and also focusing on my worth in God. But that's not always easy.

One night I was driving home from a date that went bad. The woman said, "You're a great guy, but . . ." Sure, there are a lot of things that can come after that *but*. In my mind, though, I often hear, "But you're not good-looking enough." As I was driving home that night, I prayed out of that place of frustration. Suddenly, I realized I was using the word *enough*. That stopped me in my tracks. I thought, *Is love really about being* enough *of anything?*

Well, not to God. There's nothing in the Scriptures about being holy *enough* or saved *enough* or forgiven *enough*. God's love is beyond that. I heard a great speaker once say there are three kinds of love. The first is called Love Because. We love someone *because* they're attractive or *because* they do this. The second is called Love If. We'll love someone *if* they do their hair differently or *if* they complete a task.

The third kind of love is what only God possesses: Love Period. He just loves—not *because* or *if* anything. Of course, humans can't live up to this standard of love, but what an incredible goal. This love wouldn't say, "I wish you weren't so ugly," or "I'd go out with you if you weren't bald." Instead, this love sees me with different eyes.

Hoping to be viewed with God's eyes starts by giving that gift to someone else. Like Camerin wrote, there's a lot to appreciate about someone if we look deeper and accept who that person is. Yes, this can be difficult in an appearance-obsessed culture. But let's let that be our challenge. I'm not saying, "Go find someone homely to love!" But I am saying let's pray God would reorder our priorities and help us better see with *his* eyes.

12

Biological Clock

The Parent Trap

TODD: The high school youth group boys I work with invented their own game when they got bored with less violent games like broom hockey, tackle football, and boxing. Fumble Rumble is a simple game with two rules: (1) someone holds on to an object (usually a ball, but in moments of ingenuity, the boys have used shoes, hats, and, one time, a freshman) and (2) everyone accosts that person.

One Sunday afternoon—just moments after being on the bottom of a Fumble Rumble pile and only a half hour before offering a sincere prayer for the Chicago Bears—a sophomore named Paul opened up to his small group when asked what he most wanted from life. "I want to raise a family," Paul said.

Like Paul, many men have an innate desire to be a dad—usually hidden deep down under a tough-guy image, *Simpsons'* quotes, and baseball stats. Granted, the desire is greater in some men than in others. Starting as early as preschool, I've daydreamed far more

163

about being a dad than driving a race car, pitching in game seven of the World Series, or going on a date with Jennifer Garner.

Even though men can have a strong paternal urge, we're often overlooked in cultural discussions about parental longings. You can just look at all the sitcoms and movies where dads are portrayed simply as dolts who hand out allowances and watch television, and know a guy's desire for and joy in being a dad isn't given enough credit in our culture. Let's be honest. Cuddling a baby isn't considered manly. But I'm not totally blaming culture. Instead, I think guys' parental longings are probably less realized because, well, we aren't the best at relating our feelings (surprise!). Because we seldom talk about it, I sometimes feel like I belong in a support group, shyly announcing, "Hello, my name is Todd, and I want to be a dad."

One day after church, my friend Laura was holding her baby, Natalie. I said, "I'll hold her a minute if you want to go get a drink."

"No, I'm fine," Laura said.

"Sure?"

"Yeah . . ." Laura said, somewhat perplexed.

I wasn't sure what to do at this point. I really wanted to hold Natalie. I couldn't even understand exactly why. But I didn't feel like it was kosher to just come out and admit it. On the other hand, our mutual friend Jen, who's also single, is so blatant about her desire to hold Natalie that Laura often passes the baby over like a baton as soon as Jen walks into the room. It's OK for Jen to admit she longs for a child. But for guys, that desire doesn't feel as publicly acceptable. I feel like I have to go watch a couple of eighties Schwarzenegger movies after holding an infant to regain an appropriate testosterone level.

But that day in church, I told Laura, "Um, could you act like I'm helping you? I just want to hold a baby."

OK, so I like holding babies. And I want to be someone's dad. But is my desire to be a parent as strong as the desire women feel? I don't know. I won't argue it is. But I do think it's a God-given desire, an extension of my personality type, and a male need to provide for, protect, and shape another person. I also know what I feel isn't just a feeling of "Boy, that'd be nice!"—it's a long-time longing. And as I get older, I worry more and more it won't happen. Sure, I don't have the biological timetable women do, but I also fear becoming a first-time dad late in life. My friend's dad was nearly sixty when Gene, an only child, was born. Gene's dad lived late into life, but that still meant Gene was only in his midtwenties when he had to bury his dad.

Even with all these thoughts, I still find it hard to imagine the hormones and biological urges women have. I recently heard two women in their late thirties talking about contingency plans if they don't get married soon. They both said they'll probably opt for artificial insemination. Other single women decide to adopt. But I've never even considered adoption on my own if I don't marry. So, that's my biggest sign that a woman's drive to be a mom is far greater than I can imagine. It seems like single guys instead get their pseudo-parental sense of protection, nurturing, and adventure by being an uncle, a tee-ball coach, or a youth-group counselor.

So yes, this is different than what women experience. But, I think we men can also play up or overestimate a woman's longing for kids. I've heard too many guys complain that Christian women quickly "latch" on after one date because they can hear that steady tick-tock-tick. I don't think that's generally true. In fact, I think it's funny. Guys typically don't get enough consideration for wanting to be parents, and women may get too much. That's why we need to just let members of the opposite sex—like sports fan/family man Paul—surprise us from time to time.

GOT SPERM?

Camerin: It seems ironic, or perhaps a sign of just how much things have changed in our postmodern age, that while men are now being affected by the biological clock (or are finally starting to talk about it), women are seemingly less and less affected. Most of the single women I know fall into two camps: those who want to be a mom yesterday and those who have a vague notion of wanting to be a mom . . . someday. And of the women I've spoken with about this, the majority seems to fall in the latter group.

Why? Well, that's a great question. I have a feeling the answer, as with many things associated with the modern dating scene, is multilayered and complex. I have a few theories, though, as one who also falls into this Waning Maternal Urge set. There are times I suspect this lack of urgent maternal desire is a gift from God, as there's not a lot I can do about such an urge in my current life stage (except adopting, of course, which is a huge undertaking as a single person). I also feel so busy trying to do everything in a household, from paying bills and fixing leaky faucets to cooking dinner and decorating the walls, by myself that even thinking about caring for another human being, especially a "dependent," makes me break into a cold sweat (though I know single parents miraculously perform this feat every day).

I also wonder if at times it's a defense mechanism to not desire momhood so strongly. Feeling out of the wifehood loop can be painful enough; adding the reality of being out of the momhood loop could possibly push me over the edge emotionally—so I just don't allow myself to feel that. Also, as women, so many other doors have opened for us over the past generation or two—from career to travel to ministry opportunities—that perhaps the longstanding door of becoming a mom holds less enticement. Mostly, however, I think motherhood just feels so "other" that it's tough to picture, let alone yearn for, this life stage. Most of the things that make singleness great—freedom to travel, supreme control of everything from our Daytimer to the remote, time to invest in a wide array of friends, ministry pursuits, and career opportunities—would be seriously impaired if not erased if we became a mom.

That's not to say that those of us with the Waning Maternal Urge don't love kids and want them someday. I became an aunt last year and love my little nephew to pieces. As I write this I'm planning to fly to see him (and his parents and grandparents, of course!) next weekend, and I can hardly wait to lay eyes and hugs and countless kisses on the little guy. Often when I spy cute kids or hang out with my friends' offspring, I think of a line from *Mad About You* when the main characters, Paul and Jamie, were at the pre-parenting stage. Once when they were visiting some relatives, Jamie told Paul, "Your niece is so cute it makes my uterus hurt." There are days I so get that, when I long for a little person to love on, care for, tuck into bed, and teach about everything from Jesus to shopping.

Mostly what I feel as a thirty-four-year-old single woman is a sincere hope that motherhood will be an option for me someday. That I'll get a chance at one of the most amazing of women's unique abilities: birthing new life. That there's a father-of-my-children in my future. That he'll show up before all my eggs go kaput. I've watched my sister and others go through infertility, so I know there are no guarantees at any age. And an OB/GYN friend of mine assures me that due to medical advances and the miracle that is our bodies, by and large, women even well into their forties needn't worry too much about fertility issues. But a niggling worry persists. Mostly in that very American part of me that sees biological motherhood as some sort of inalienable right and that will be altogether indignant (and grief stricken) if I'm denied what seems to come so easily to others, even unsuspecting teenagers in backseats of cars.

I read a chick-lit novel several years ago called *Dating Big Bird* in which the main character, a still-single woman, described the ticking biological clock not as sand in an hourglass (which can simply be turned over when it's run out) but as a big gumball machine with a limited number of gumballs slipping out one by one. Once they're gone, that's it. No more eggs. No more chance for a baby. Sometimes, when I spy a cute kid, or watch a meaningful mother-child moment, or just for no foreseeable reason whatsoever, the maternal pang hits and I feel like a grubby, penniless kid with my nose pressed against the glass of that gumball machine, eyeing the slowly disappearing treats, hoping for the needed "currency" before they're all gone.

So what does all this have to do with dating? Well, if a date-potential happens to catch me on one of those gumball-machine days, I can view him with everything from contempt—as in "You're late! Your bad timing is why I'll never be able to become a mom!"—to desperation—"Please share your life, and sperm, with me!" Dating, as you've gathered by this point in the book, is complicated enough without our whacked-out hormones or Baby Lust factoring into the equation. I don't want my waning egg count to speed up a dating relationship. And I want to truly consider whether a guy would make a good father, not just whether or not he's physically capable of making me a mom. I also sometimes fear that Paternal Urge-y guys will view my age as a liability and will opt for a younger woman, which just makes me want to scream.

More often than not, however, a date-potential will catch me on my more numerous Waning Maternal Urge days. And this new trend for single women can alarm or confuse guys. A friend of mine almost suffered a breakup with her boyfriend of many months when he discovered she wasn't dying to become a mom. She, like many modern single women, had that "someday it'll probably be nice to be somebody's mother" feeling. In his mind, this translated into *no* interest in momhood, and that worried him, since he really wanted to be a dad. It took a good deal of conversation, as with many things when it comes to male-female communication, to help them realize they're basically on the same track.

WHAT DO WE DO ABOUT IT?

TODD: In the midst of several hard conversations that led to a breakup, I noticed a trend. My then-girlfriend kept repeating what I thought was one of those sincere compliments paid during a healthy breakup. She said often, "You'll be such a good dad."

I didn't think much of it at first. I mean, I was saying things like, "We've had so much fun," and "You're a great friend." Then, I realized her repeated line wasn't just a compliment. Nor was it really about my potential fatherhood skills. Instead, this was a nagging thought as she was processing our breakup. She knew we were splitting for legitimate reasons, but she just couldn't let go of one idea: *This is a chance to have a family.* And she was watching it disappear.

This was the first time I saw the power of the desire to have a family. That desire isn't necessarily a negative, but both genders have to be aware of the role it plays. Yes, we date to find a spouse and—God willing—a partner in parenting, but of course we can't just pick *anyone* who carries the needed set of chromosomes. My then-girlfriend, knowing the relationship didn't fit with what God wanted for each of us, was obviously torn. With a few different variables, maybe we would have stayed together, mostly fueled by our mutual desire to have kids. But, it wouldn't have been right.

Of course, people settle for less than God's best in romantic relationships for various reasons. But for never-marrieds who are getting older and for singles looking for a spouse to help parent existing children, there's an especially pervasive little voice saying, *This one's good enough. Go for it.*

I've seen my desire for children cloud my thinking when looking for a spouse. Tag-teaming with my desire to not be alone, the desire to have kids has pushed me to remain in relationships I shouldn't have and ask out women not based on our chemistry but her availability and potential as a mom. Besides that, I face a whirlwind of questions when considering a woman I'm interested in. What do I do if after a year of dating she announces she doesn't want kids? What if she isn't sure whether or not she wants children? How do I balance my hopes for fatherhood, a woman's desire to be a mom, and God's leading when making decisions about dating?

For me, I think the key to discerning the answers to all these questions is honesty: honesty in the relationship, honesty with myself, and honesty with God. You really have to look at your intentions—and hers—and be honest about what you see. With God, I try to be open about my motivations and pray for wisdom and discernment. In the relationship, openness is just as important—especially in the beginning. I know, you don't want to open the first date with, "So, do you want kids?" But I've found it good to at least broach the topic in the first few months in order to save great heartache later on. Then, once the commitment grows, so can the specifics of this discussion.

Sometimes, it's hard to really evaluate whether you're practicing all this needed honesty. This is why observant, trustworthy, and frank friends are necessary (in addition to older, mature married couples who can guide and mentor). Ask these trusted friends to look for internal pressure on the relationship and to be honest with you—even if you don't want to hear it.

DATING . . . WITH CHILDREN

Camerin: Sometimes the complicating issue in a dating relationship isn't the absence of kids but the presence of them. Namely, kids from a previous marriage, or relationship, or rendezvous. It's difficult enough with two people in a relationship, but when you add kids who've suffered a divorce or death of a parent, who may or may not be keen on their mom/dad dating you, who may get attached to you too quickly or fear attachment because you, too, might leave, things can get *really* complicated. That doesn't even factor in the former spouse, who's a permanent fixture in the lives of these kids and your date.

Years ago I had a tough conversation with a friend who was agonizing over her relationship with the man she was seriously dating. He had three kids from a previous marriage, all of them of junior-high-school age and younger. He had custody of them every other weekend, which meant if she married him, she would become an instant mom. While she loved this man dearly and was excited about the prospect of becoming his wife, she wasn't sure if she was ready for the throes of motherhood at the age of twenty-five. She was seriously torn about how to proceed.

Another friend of mine, Joy, dated an older man off and on for many years before eventually marrying him when she was thirty-one. At the time, he had a college-age daughter who presented an interesting challenge for Joy. The daughter obviously didn't need much hands-on parenting, which left Joy with the awkward task of figuring out how to factor in to the young woman's life. And the ex-wife only made all of their lives miserable. For the first few years of their marriage, Joy and her new husband had to adjust not only to each other and to married life but also to these two other people spinning in and out of their orbit on a regular basis. On many occasions, Joy was quite open with me about just how challenging this was. Did she regret marrying in to this sometimes-sticky situation? No way. She loves her hubby and her new life dearly. But this extra cast of characters hasn't exactly made this new chapter of her life smooth and easy.

They say when you marry someone you marry their entire family. While this is usually a warning to carefully check out your potential in-laws, in the case of kids and exes, this truism is especially crucial to consider. These people *will* be a part of your new life together, for better or for worse. Going in eyes wide open will at least spare you the surprise of these complications. While it's always important to remember that dating involves people's hearts and to make all communication, actions, and decisions accordingly, with the case of children, it's our responsibility as the adults to remember that these are young, tender, and often bruised hearts we're dealing with. Their health needs to be one of the most important considerations.

I found it interesting, and quite telling, that when I asked the readers of my singles column who have children or have dated someone with children about guidelines for dating with kids in the mix, I received answers all over the map. I heard from a mom of four who's waiting until her kids are out of the house to date again, and from another single mom who wants her daughter to see her in a healthy romantic relationship so she can model what one looks like. I heard from a woman who still has a relationship with an ex-boyfriend's four-year-old son, and others who regret getting so attached to the children now that the relationship's over.

All to say there are no formulas here. As with many things in the single life, I think it's important to know yourself and your strengths and weaknesses and take those into consideration when creating any boundaries. And it's obviously crucial to be in close relationship with God, who knows us, our dates, any children in the mix, to know how best to proceed in any romantic relationship. In these instances we're reminded of how much we need God, and how blessed we are to be able to lean on his all-knowing, all-wise, higher ways.

13

Intergender Friendships

Risks, Rewards, and Recreational Kissing— Is It Really That Weird?

TODD: It was one of those moments like you see in old Westerns when a ruffian (usually named Black Bart) calls the sheriff out for a gunfight. As the lawman decides how to respond—walk away, be civil, or draw his gun—everything falls silent. Everyone turns their eyes to the action.

But in my case, the ruffian used a tactic worse than any of Black Bart's. One of my friends, in front of at least ten other people, asked me, "So why are you and Stacy just friends?" Everyone was staring at me. I was starting to sweat. My hand crept down to my belt to reveal I hadn't worn my six-shooter that day.

Only a few weeks later, I watched the same attack launched on a friend, Allison. Like me, Allison wasn't armed. Unlike me, she came up with a response more coherent than awkward stammering. She responded, "Because we're *friends*."

Simple, but it also says a lot. For some reason, there seems to be the idea that male-female friendships are secondary to a romantic relationship. When someone asks why you're *just* friends, they imply that the goal is romance first and friendship second. Friendship becomes like a default function: "If I'm not attracted to you, then we'll just be friends."

I believe there are people who are custom-fitted friends, which is a valuable role in our life journey and walk with Christ. I've seen proof of this in my male friendships—pseudo-brothers whom I'm convinced God has blessed me with to help support me, enrich me, and teach me the intricacies of the curveball. I don't think this role is gender-specific (well, maybe the curveball part).

Yes, there are complications in developing close friendships with the other gender. The biggest obstacle is obviously that a deep emotional intimacy can blur the line between friendship and romance. It's probably this messiness that scares some people into an all or nothing approach: either you're dating and picking out curtains (all), or you're not having a close relationship with the other gender at all (nothing).

I believe there's a middle ground. In my life, close female friends are nearly indispensable. Why?

A year or two ago I broke up with a girl I'd only been seeing for a short time. But still, I was in need of comfort and sympathy. I told my friend Mike what happened, and he said, "Wow, that relationship was quicker than Rasheed Wallace's career as an Atlanta Hawk!"

That's not exactly what I was looking for. And no, this is by far not the limit of male empathy, but I know this: in a post-breakup debriefing, no woman would *ever* bring up basketball player Rasheed Wallace (who played for Atlanta for just one game before being traded to the Detroit Pistons). Instead, a woman will typically lend advice, support, and affirmation beyond a punch on the arm.

Here are the thoughts of one man in his forties about similar hardships he's found:

> Like women, men also crave companionship, a partner to go through life with. In fact, we may be worse off than single women, because they can depend on their friends for emotional support, whereas most guys will not discuss feelings, or heaven forbid, let us be sad or cry in front of them. A romantic partner is about the only one with whom we can experience emotional closeness.

Guy friends are great. And yes, they do offer support and advice, but I feel like they're half of the puzzle. Female friends can bring the sensitivity and touchy-feeliness to a friendship that a man won't always find with guy buddies. Besides that, I know I need women friends to tell me when I'm wearing shoes that don't match my pants. Oh, and they also can help me better understand the female mind. I mean, when traveling in an unknown country, who's a better tour guide than a native?

As for women, I'm sure us guys are indispensable as friends too. You know, to explain the art of the curveball.

GUESS WHAT? MEN AND WOMEN ARE DIFFERENT

Camerin: I don't think I've ever talked about curveballs with any of my male friends, but these guys certainly have proven essential in my life just the same. So much so that I'd call opposite-sex friends one of the secrets of singlehood success.

Why are these friends so important? Each gender brings their own unique blessings and benefits into friendships. So if all our friends are our own gender, we're missing out on a whole lot of blessings. And if we fall into the all-or-nothing camp, it's easy to get desperate for opposite-gender presence in our life—and therefore less discerning when contemplating whether or not to develop a relationship with someone.

I've found six other reasons opposite-gender friends are a must-have—both to your personal life *and* your dating life.

They bring different gifts to the table. From a female's perspective, this often translates to muscle and mechanical know-how. For example, my friend Tim helps me install my mondo-heavy window air conditioner every spring. Not only does he have the muscle to heft the monstrosity to my window, he also knows how to secure it there so it won't fall out on the heads of any unsuspecting passersby. One techie-friend went with me to select my laptop computer, to help me figure out which bells and whistles I really needed and, more importantly, needed to pay for. Todd has mentioned that women in his life have offered fashion advice, and I've helped other guys shop for and decorate their homes. Sure, some people's strengths defy gender stereotypes. I know some guys who could teach me a few things in the kitchen. But by and large, people of the opposite gender often come equipped with strengths very different from our own. And when we let them into our lives via friendship, we're the better for it.

They remind us that men and women really are different. This is a lesson I learned the hard way with my friend Max. Poor guy, I used to call him when I needed someone to listen to my tirade about life's ills or my excitement about my latest accomplishment. Proto-male that he is, instead of sympathizing or celebrating, he tried to fix the problem or challenge me to accomplish even more. Once I realized I was erroneously expecting him to play the role of another girlfriend in my life, I was freed to appreciate the role he was created to play. Now I call him when I need to chew over a problem or brainstorm how to tackle a new project. I so appreciate his unique perspective. And through our friendship I have a better grasp on what to realistically expect from men. We women especially can get so frustrated expecting the men in our life to play the role of a girlfriend. And while some men certainly may be wired in ways that lend to that kind of relationship, most of the males of the species were created different from us on purpose. And allowing them to operate in those differences in our friendships hopefully will prepare us to allow them to operate in them in our romantic relationships as well.

They can introduce us to their friends! I'll never forget the email I received years ago from Henry, a co-worker friend whose wife, Helene, I'd started developing a good friendship with as well (another opposite-gender friendship blessing!). To my memory, the email went something like this:

```
Camerin:
    So, um, how are you? Nice weather we're
having, eh?
    Sheesh, I don't know how to do this
without sounding like a dithering old
aunt: "I know this nice young man . . ."
    So I'll just come right out with it.
I have a friend Helene thinks you'd hit
it off with. Maybe we could all go out
together sometime, if you're interested.
Your call.
```

After I finished giggling over this email, I replied that as long as Helene thought this was a reasonably well-thought-out match, I was game. We all went out a week or two later—to a casual weekend lunch. Though nothing came of this outing, it was nice to have another option to consider . . . and another guy just to get to know.

It stands to reason that opposite-gender friends probably have more friends of their same gender. And some of them have to be single. So foster those other-sex friendships, reap their benefits, and you just might get the chance to work your way into the hearts of *their* friends.

They keep us from stereotyping and gender-bashing. When I went out with a guy a few years back who was slow to initiate and commit in our relationship, it was tempting, in my resulting frustration, to think *all* men are like that—and to whine as such. But due to my friendship with Todd, who in the previous six months had asked out two different women he was interested in, I couldn't make these sweeping claims. In previous chapters, Todd and I have already beat the drum repeatedly about how much we singles are guilty of generalizing—often in a negative light—the opposite gender. One surefire antidote to that bad habit is having a few friends who keep the other gender from being the *them* in the us vs. them syndrome.

They help us narrow down what we need in a potential partner. A friend of a friend once relayed to me that during a dating drought, she prayed for God to grant her more male friends. Apparently, he provided—and she learned a lot from this. "I admired many qualities about these men as I got to know them probably better than I would have if we'd been in a dating relationship and mired in emotional drama, physical boundary issues, and such," she said. "When all of those factors were gone, I could see a clearer picture of the type of man that God might have for me as a husband someday."

They remind us that all people have value. When you desire to be in a romantic relationship, it's easy to see each person of the other gender as either Dating Potential or Not Dating Potential, and to ascribe them value accordingly. But, as Christians, we know this isn't how we're supposed to treat our brothers and sisters, who are all created in God's image, are all fearfully and wonderfully made, and some of whom need to be in our life as friends so that we're functioning in a well-rounded community and body of believers.

THE CONFUSING GAME OF "FRIEND OR MORE?"

TODD: Late one night in college, I sat in the library with a close friend, laughing and sharing stories. As I listened to Jennifer share about an embarrassing moment, I suddenly realized how much fun I was having and how comfortable I felt. And that got me thinking about the nature of our relationship. During the next lull in conversation, I told her, "I'm so glad that ever since I've known you, you've had a boyfriend you're going to marry."

"Why?" she said.

"Because we can just enjoy our friendship without any of that awkward 'should we date or shouldn't we?' junk."

"Yeah," she said. "It saved us a lot of crap."

Jennifer was truly one of those God-fitted friends who meant a lot to me. I was never romantically attracted to her. But, on nights like this—with lots of closeness and fun—I could've gotten confused. That "what if?" question would pop up. I'd hear that little voice: *You know? Here's a good woman right here!* But without a romantic relationship as even an option, Jennifer and I were able to simply relax and enjoy our friendship.

Of course, even with the existence of Boyfriend Mark, our friendship wasn't a cakewalk. There are still dangers that intergender friends can fall prey to—whether the friends are single, dating others, or are married. Jennifer and I had to create concrete emotional boundaries to honor her relationship—and safeguard our hearts. We had some basic guidelines: (1) We hung out together

179

but rarely was it just the two of us. In fact, I can't think of any situation that could have been confused as a date. (2) We'd discuss things happening in our lives but no deep secrets or passions that would make either of us emotionally vulnerable.

These boundaries haven't always held up in my intergender relationships. I'll admit I've gotten confused. I've gotten too emotionally involved. I've developed crushes that in hindsight I realize were based more on convenience and comfort than true feelings. I can't speak for women, but I know guys can fall into a harmful "why not" thinking. If we're feeling close to a woman—even if our relationship is strictly friendship—we start thinking romance because, well, it's an option. And it's convenient: no pickup lines, no searching, no loneliness. Of course, this is not a trend limited to men, but I think we more easily fall into this trap because we don't have a lot of intimate relationships. So when we have one, we think, *This isn't what I'm used to; it must be something other than friendship.*

Another contributing factor could be our visually oriented nature. I'll admit that with close female friends whom I find attractive, it can be even easier to say, "Why not?" Also, guys are fixers and want to "win a beauty" as John Eldredge says in *Wild at Heart*, so if we're close to a woman who longs for a romantic option, we want to be that for her. I'd like to challenge men—like I've had to challenge myself—to really analyze and pray over friendships before pursuing more. Why am I drawn to her? Are my feelings about convenience and what *I* can get out of the relationship? Or are they about what would be best for God and her?

There are no easy answers. Jana wrote to ChristianSinglesToday.com with a good example of a friendship that survived despite complications:

```
I met Peter in college, and we hit it
off instantly. I learned a lot from Peter
```

180

and identified in him qualities I now want
in a future spouse. I considered it a gift
to have a glimpse into how the male mind
works. I never considered him as more
than a friend—from the very beginning we
somehow built a healthy boundary. However,
once there was a time when we were getting
too emotionally close and I had to step
back a bit. But he honored that, and our
friendship survived and even thrived.

DANGER, WILL ROBINSON!

Camerin: While, as Todd mentioned, there are no easy answers here, I do think there are some basic guidelines to healthy,
happy male-female friendships. I also think there are some needed
warnings.

Married Friends—Last spring after my married friend Tim had
just installed my window air conditioner and we were in a local
coffee shop where I was treating him to our traditional Thanks a
Bunch Frappuccino, the topic of appropriate male-female friendships arose. It came up in the context of some mutual friends of
ours, but in agreeing with Tim's cautious stance, I said, "Well, of
course you know I wouldn't even dream of sitting here with you
if Michelle didn't know we're here or if she felt any sort of unease
about our friendship." Though I was pretty sure Tim was aware of
my own cautious stance on male-female friendships when one or
more of the parties are married, it was good to verbalize it. And,
as always, I sent him home with a frap for Michelle too.

In a similar fashion, I have a male co-worker who brings up
his wife, always in a flattering light, in almost every conversation
I have with him. While there are times I want to say, "I get it,
you're married" or "You know, I'm not attracted to you, so you
don't have to worry," I still understand and appreciate that he's

keeping our interactions in a larger context. His wife is always there with us.

For all the importance and benefits of intergender friendships, these relationships are still altogether eclipsed by the importance of the marriage. I've learned it's wise to keep all conversations or get-togethers very open and very public. If the spouse is at all uncomfortable with your friendship, bail. If your married friend starts confiding in you about problems with his or her spouse or the marriage in general, create some emotional distance between you two. And if you ever start to feel attracted to your married friend, stop, drop, and roll on out of there because you're playing with fire. It also wouldn't hurt to share your feelings with a trusted friend who can keep you accountable.

Single Friends—Todd's already pointed out the danger of moving from friendship to romance for all the wrong reasons—convenience, familiarity, comfort, desperation. But how do you discern right motivations for this transition from wrong ones? Personally, I've found a one-word question extremely helpful: *why?* When I start to have those "Hmm, what about him?" thoughts about one of my guy friends, I've found it's important to look at *why* I'm having those thoughts. A couple years back I started this line of wondering about my friend Ryan after discussing a struggle I was going through. He was genuinely helpful—listening well and offering kind comments. But when I was totally honest with myself about the resulting "hmm" feeling afterward, I realized it was more about the emotional closeness we'd just shared than it was about *him*. And the next time we chatted about normal stuff, I realized the "hmm" was nowhere in sight.

Another key to the success of intergender friendships is complete honesty. And this starts inside our own heads. Every now and then when a guy friend of mine has started dating someone, I've felt an unmistakable twinge of jealousy. Not just in that "I wish *I* was dating someone" kind of way, or the "I'm going to have to share you with someone now" kind of way, but in the "I wish it was me dating you" kind of way. It's then I realize I haven't been completely honest with myself about how I really feel about the guy. Of course, then I also have to go back and make sure these are real romantic feelings and not pseudo-romantic feelings, as mentioned above. A good gut-check every now and then in relationships is asking yourself, honestly, if your friend were to start dating someone tomorrow, how would you feel? And why? Is it always that simple? No way! This is complicated terrain. But this question can at least help you get started in figuring out the lay of the land.

Why is this brutal self-honesty so important? Because if we have a secret crush on our other-gender friend (sometimes secret even to ourselves), we can get lulled into unhealthy emotional dependence that prevents us from getting close to potential dates—which isn't fair to us—or that creates all kinds of weirdness when the other person starts to date someone—which isn't fair to our friend.

It's also vital to be honest with each other. If you're feeling genuine attraction, you know you're eventually going to have to spill it. And if you sense your friend is crushing on you, it's irresponsible to stay silent. It's one thing to unwittingly lead someone on, but when you sense he or she is digging on you, it's only right to create some distance or bring it out in the open. Potentially awkward? Yes. But also the most respectful thing you can do for your friend and your friendship.

IF YOU CAN'T BE WITH THE ONE YOU LOVE . . .

Camerin: The final caution? Well, it's not one you hear discussed often in Christian circles, but I know it affects us. It's the NCMO (Non-Committal Make Out) or FWB (Friend With Benefits). It's when dates are in short supply and hormones are multiplying like rabbits. It's those times when you can't remember the last time you kissed someone and, well, that friend of yours has lips.

I hate to admit it, but I fell victim to this one years ago. My guy friend Sam had just suffered a messy breakup, and I was in the middle of a dating dry spell. We'd always exchanged flirty banter in our years of friendship and had even experienced seasons when one or the other of us was interested in "more than friendship," though usually during times when the one on the receiving end of the affection was unavailable for one reason or another. So, when we finally got our single seasons in synch, and were both feeling a bit lonely one night when we were watching a movie at my place, we kissed.

Was it fun at the moment? You bet. Was it awkward later? Big time! In fact, we didn't talk for two weeks while I tried to recover from the weirdness and attempt to figure out what to say, where to go from there. It's one thing to purposely transition from friendship to romance or even to allow it to transition through something like a kiss. But to just give in to hormones because you're lonely and the other person is there (and admittedly, there's a context of caring) certainly doesn't honor your friend, yourself, or God's guidelines for healthy relationships. In the end, the damage this did to our friendship wasn't worth the temporary rush those kisses provided. Since then, I've learned to avoid being alone with Sam when I'm in one of those needing-to-reaffirm-my-womanhood moods. And when I'm needing more physical contact, I try to hang out with my toddler nephew or go get a pedicure.

WORTH IT?

 TODD: OK, let me note for the guys out there that I, like you, don't go get a pedicure when I'm feeling like smooching. (Come to think of it, I don't even *understand* how getting your toenails clipped stands in for romantic contact.) But I understand what

Camerin's saying. A lot of what we both feel about intergender friendships comes down to stepping back, getting perspective, and carefully and truthfully weighing our feelings. But is it worth it? It sure is—maybe just so we guys can learn why a pedicure can sub in for making out.

14

Breaking Up

The Remains of the Date

Camerin: My worst breakup: I was at an out-of-state Christian music festival with a group of old college friends. In the parking lot. While Christian singer Susan Ashton was singing "There's a Grand Canyon between you and me." And it was my birthday weekend.

I'm not making this up. Really. I couldn't make this kind of stuff up. To top it all off, the seven-hour drive home alone was so tear-filled and blurry that I had to pull over and take a quick, uncomfortable nap at a rest stop.

In short, breakups suck. They can break our heart, jeopardize our self-esteem, and make us wonder where on earth God is in all the mess. But for Christians, we who are instructed to treat one another with love and respect and who trust in God's sovereignty, surely this process doesn't have to be so fraught with anguish.

Is there such a thing as a Christian rejection, breakup, or relationship with an ex? Does having an everlasting Lover of our soul take away some of the sting of good-bye? These are difficult questions indeed, considering that for us singles, every romantic relationship we've been in has ended.

FOR WHEN I AM WEAK, THEN I AM STRONG

TODD: In all this messiness, all the anguish, and all these questions, I think believers have something that sets us apart in the dating game: hope.

All romantic relationships are made up of two people with an eye toward what's best for them and what's best for their partner. But a Christian relationship adds a third consideration. Believers first and foremost look for *God's* best to be done. It gives me great hope to think of a girlfriend as a fellow traveler in the faith journey—even in a breakup. Why? First, it means that for all the screwy things I do and say, I'm extended the grace, respect, and an unconditional love that comes from being viewed with God's eyes. Second, I'm able to view the relationship as a mutual process of discerning God's will. Instead of self-blame, doubt, or finger-pointing, I try to realize that for some reason, this just wasn't God's best for me.

Of course, I don't want to be all sunshine and rainbows here. The business of breaking up sure isn't when I can best see God's hand or plan. But deep down, even when it seems as if God is terribly far away, I know he's faithful. I might not get what I want when I want it, but all I can do is trust and hope to do God's will. Sound hard? It is.

In his book *Thoughts in Solitude*, Trappist monk Thomas Merton admits to God that not only does he not know his own path, but he can't even *see* the road in front of him. Merton was trying to do God's will but honestly didn't know whether he was or not. His hope, though, was that his mere effort to please God would please God. The last lines of the prayer say this:

Therefore I will trust you always, though I may seem to be lost
and in the shadow of death.
I will not fear, for you are ever with me, and you will never leave
me to face my perils alone.[18]

The truth is, we can't always understand why failed relationships happen. We can't always spot God during hardships. Instead, like Merton, we can only hand it all over to God and trust in his greater purpose.

It's hard to remember God is always with us when he feels distant. It may be harder to remember he can use our pain and weakness when it makes no sense to us. In his second letter to the Corinthians, Paul wrote,

Three times I pleaded with the Lord to take [my thorn] from me. But he said to me, "My grace is sufficient for you, for my power is made perfect in weakness." . . . That is why, for Christ's sake, I delight in weaknesses, in insults, in hardships, in persecutions, in difficulties. For when I am weak, then I am strong.

12:8–10

DEALING AND HEALING

TODD: In suffering and surviving breakups, there are three lessons I've had to learn:

1. It's OK to feel. After a girlfriend broke up with me a few years ago, my initial response could've been summed up with, "Eh, oh well." It wasn't just an act I put on to be Mr. Tough Guy. I literally felt very little grief, loss, or sadness.

After a week, a friend said, "You know, it's OK to be sad." *But I'm really not*, I thought. When I got thinking about it, I realized

I'd subconsciously held the broken relationship at arm's length so I wouldn't have to deal with the messiness.

Of course, my gender may be the chief culprit for my lack of emotional awareness. But I think there are cultural messages also at work that can make any of us more guarded with our emotions. First of all, no one wants to be messy, and it's quite clear from culture (and often the church as well) that no one really wants us to be messy around them either. We feel like we need to have it all together and be content all the time.

On top of that, I often feel like I don't deserve to be down or sad over a breakup. A few years ago I told my mostly married Bible study group how torn up I was because of a breakup. Before I knew it, I was backpedaling from my revelation because their reactions made me feel like my dating woes were insignificant. They couldn't relate, and so I thought, *Well, I guess compared to the day-to-day struggles of marriage, the demise of my little three-month relationship isn't really a big deal.*

Obviously, the end of any relationship isn't insignificant. It's OK to be sad. I've taken three steps (besides prayer) to teach myself how.

Somehow, find a release. When my grandfather died, I didn't cry at all for about a month after his death. And then I saw the film *Big Fish.* I started tearing up because of the moving story, but when my tears turned into all-out bawling, I realized I was no longer crying about the movie. After a recent tearless breakup, I popped in a reliable tearjerker for me, *Remember the Titans.* Long after the Titans won the big game, I was still releasing pain, sadness, and frustration with God.

Be messy with someone. I feel like I can be messy around my friends simply because I allow them to be messy. In fact, Camerin, our friend LaTonya, and I have formed an unofficial support group of sorts. We take turns providing sappy movies and chocolate (for the girls) or big pasta-filled meals and fun toys (for me) during times of sadness. More importantly, we give each other a green light for messiness, irrational comments, and neediness. Having someone you know you can be real with (and who prays for you and offers compassion) is mandatory.

Know God cares. I used to think God would see me whining about a broken relationship and roll his eyes. Or I'd blame him for being responsible. But the movie *Signs* made me rethink God's presence whenever I hurt. In the film, a boy is suffering an asthma attack and his father cradles him on his lap and says, "I know it hurts. It will pass. Believe it will pass. Just wait. Don't be afraid. Believe." I love to think that's exactly what God says to me in painful times.

2. It's OK to need time. Whenever I'm post-breakup, I imagine people whispering, "Boy, he isn't over it *yet*?" Of course, I'm sure that usually no one is thinking that, but I need to remind myself that it's normal to need time. How long? Well, that's what's tricky; depending on the length and intensity of the relationship and the messiness of the breakup, the recovery time varies. There's no magic formula.

So I fall back on two things to help me gauge my recovery: (1) I need to pray for patience and for God to help me allow myself to grieve. (2) I need friends to let me mourn and talk things out with to make sure I'm not wallowing in pity or rushing through healing. I trust them to be honest with me and ask me questions about what I'm feeling. And they can help me gauge whether or not my grief is healthy.

3. It's OK to want someone. In Jennifer Croley's book on surviving divorce, *Missing Being Mrs.*, she says that when her marriage ended, a lot of her friends told her, "Well, at least you've got God." This made her feel incredibly guilty to feel lonely. Finally, she prayed about it. God reminded her of what he says in Genesis 2:18: "It's not good for . . . man to be alone." But realizing *when* God said this to Adam made all the difference to Jennifer. She writes:

He was in the Garden of Eden, in *paradise*, with everything he needed, before the fall, when he was still in full, constant, walking, talking fellowship with *God*. And even then God himself says, "It's not good for man to be alone." . . . Human beings need God. They also need other human beings. God himself says so. So don't feel bad if you feel lonely. . . . [God] knows it's not good for you to be alone too much.[19]

Jennifer's right: God made us to want other humans, so we should cut ourselves some slack. Of course, we can't wallow in our loneliness. Or turn our search for a spouse into an idol where our desire for "the one" grows almost more intense than our desire for God. But we need to remember God knows what's best for us because he made us.

WHEN GOD SAYS NO

Camerin: Many years ago, I suffered the worst heartbreak of my life. I'd been dating Andrew off and on for three years, and I knew we needed to make a decision to move forward or move on. Despite the fact I'd met him at church on Valentine's Day, that he made me laugh and made me feel beautiful, that he loved God and loved his family, I still couldn't get any peace about moving toward marriage with this terrific guy. I prayed—no, pleaded—with God for direction. And when I was met with silence and a lack of peace for months on end, I slowly, excruciatingly let this relationship go.

Without a tangible reason for the breakup, it was easy to question the wisdom of this decision in the years following. There were no "irreconcilable differences" or "I want kids and he doesn't" type issues to blame, only a vague sense that God said no. I alternated between seasons of peace (which thankfully grew longer over the years) and seasons of waning trust in God's grand plan.

I wasn't obsessing, just wondering what to do with that nagging question mark in the back of my mind. God had a subtle response for that too.

I was on a shopping excursion with my roommate several years later when I saw my ex-boyfriend across a trendy furniture store. He was with a woman. Even though I hadn't talked to Andrew or seen him in years, I failed to muster the courage to say hello.

Later, kicking myself for being such a chicken, I chatted with God about this "chance" encounter. "Were you wanting us to get back in contact, God? Was it just bad timing before?" The what-ifs crept in big time, and I once again prayed for peace and direction. I remember thinking that it would almost be a relief to know he was married. It would put the issue to rest once and for all.

Well, a few months later, I had another "chance" encounter. This time with a woman from my Bible study. We were chatting about work when it somehow came up that she knew Andrew. She'd even dated him briefly. She still saw him on occasion at work and knew that he'd just gotten married a few weeks before.

I stood there in stunned silence, an odd mixture of grief and peace washing over me. It was the peace of a closed door and the loneliness of an empty horizon all at once. And amazement at the way God had orchestrated this answer to my prayer. It was a difficult yet unmistakable reminder that God has it all in control—breakups and weddings, what-ifs and answers to prayer, and someday, if it's in his plan, the arrival of my Mr. Right. Though he didn't have to, though I should know better by now, God once again proved his trustworthiness to me.

In the years since that painful, seemingly nonsensical breakup, I've also become a singles columnist, author, and speaker. I've been able to use the pain of that situation and the resulting singleness to reach out to my fellow singletons. And it's been a rich journey indeed. Even if the breakup wasn't God's will, he's redeemed the situation—and blessed my socks off with the cool singles I've met and interesting places I've traveled in my gig as SingleWoman.

Similarly, a woman we once featured in *Today's Christian Woman* magazine (where I'm on the editorial staff) agonizingly watched her husband walk out of her life. Years later she birthed a ministry to newly divorced women by opening her home to these hurting souls, providing a respite and escape from this tough, unwanted life transition. (As a side note: she met her second husband through this ministry as well—the photographer we sent to shoot a picture of her to go with the article!)

Again, when we allow him to, once the initial shock and essential grieving process have subsided, God can scoop up the shreds of our heart and dreams and not only patch us up but also craft something altogether new and beautiful in the process. He doesn't waste a thing. And therein lies our unique and wonderful hope as Christians in a world full of breakups, death, and rejection. No matter what we endure, God is always bigger than our heartache and is always sovereign.

THE EX-FILES

Camerin: There's a scenario that used to repeat itself every now and then when I'd eat out with girlfriends. Someone would order a dish that came with fries, they'd struggle with the ketchup bottle, and I'd brag that I knew the secret of extracting this condiment from its stubborn container. I'd valiantly take the bottle and hit the neck hard with the heel of my hand. Then I'd smile wide as the red stuff flowed freely on my friend's plate.

"Where'd you learn that?" someone would inevitably ask, to which I always responded, "I learned it from an old boyfriend. It's hands-down the best thing I got out of the relationship." Then we all would laugh—and occasionally launch into ex-boyfriend bashing.

Let's face it, anyone who's been single for a number of years has experienced more than their share of pain and rejection at the hands of people they cared about, whether those people meant to hurt them or not.

My friends and I laugh often about the Fence Breaker, the guy who drove into my friend Julie's fence when he went to pick her up for their first and only date and never made good on his promise to fix it. On a more serious note, I constantly remind another friend that she deserves someone so much better than her ex of four years. He had more issues than the magazine section of Borders, yet he dragged *her* to counseling for a little fixing up.

While these sometimes-hurtful behaviors are so easy to see, what's sometimes harder to glimpse through our pain is the good in our exes. No matter how someone may have treated us, he or she is still one of God's creations, and his fingerprints are in there (Eph. 2:10).

Convicted by my funny, yet not-so-Christlike Ketchup Queen act, I made an effort to see the good qualities in my exes, the things that drew me to them in the first place. With God's help I've come to realize the guy who undermined my self-esteem with his constant sarcastic comments also helped birth my love for travel. And the old flame who broke my heart by dumping me on my birthday also made me feel beautiful for the first time in my life. Seeing the good in these guys, savoring the great memories of our time together, and thanking God for the positives amidst the negatives has led me to a less jaded, more hopeful outlook. And one that pleases God.

Don't get me wrong, I'm not making excuses for hurtful behavior—especially abuse, which is never, ever OK. And there are times we set ourselves up for pain by walking into relationships we have no business entering. But holding a grudge usually just ends up hurting *us*. Looking for the good in a past relationship may seem like a Pollyanna-like exercise, but it yields amazing benefits: happier, healthier singlehood.

So now whenever I'm the ketchup hero at dinner with friends, I simply say, "I learned that trick from an old boyfriend. He was really handy like that." I may be missing a good laugh, but I and everyone at my table gain a more positive perspective about the opposite gender specifically and relationships in general.

WHAT WE WANT IN A NO

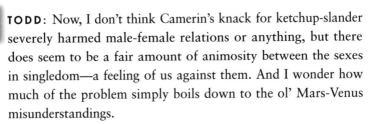

TODD: Now, I don't think Camerin's knack for ketchup-slander severely harmed male-female relations or anything, but there does seem to be a fair amount of animosity between the sexes in singledom—a feeling of us against them. And I wonder how much of the problem simply boils down to the ol' Mars-Venus misunderstandings.

Case in point: for guys, a lot of pain and bitterness toward women come out of being rejected when asking a woman for the first date. The thing is, the answer isn't always the biggest problem. It's the way it's delivered.

To be honest, I don't envy a woman when she's asked out and, for whatever reason, has to say no. I honestly don't know how I'd respond (although it may involve running away), so I actually can't blame women for *anything* they say in turning us down. Besides, I think they're honestly trying to make it go easier, but something gets lost in the translation between Female Dialect and Male Dialect. The worst horror story I've heard is the man who heard this: "I want to marry a guy just like you. Just not you."

So what do guys want from a no? Doing informal research with friends, I found some interesting patterns to help give some guidance.

Be honest. Be clear. This may seem like a no-brainer, but guys want honesty. That doesn't mean we want you to reveal every detail and say, "Well, you're a lot chunkier than I normally like." Instead, just be clear and direct. "I'm not interested" or "I'm not attracted to you" works fine. Don't waffle, try too hard to be nice, drag it out, or leave room for us to think that maybe you'll change your mind. Give it to us straight. (Of course, if the invitation comes from a friend, the situation is different, and I'll get to that.)

Don't flatter us. I know women probably say things like "You're a great guy, but . . ." to genuinely be nice. But that's not what guys hear. The male mind automatically thinks, "If I was so great you'd say yes, so you must be lying."

We also focus on the "but." You could say two hundred nice things about us, but we'd walk away and go, "I guess I wasn't _____ enough." We'll fill in the blank with whatever we aren't comfortable with about ourselves. I remember once getting a flattering rejection saying I was funny and sweet and smart. *If I'm all those things*, I thought, *then what's the problem? It must be that I'm ugly.* Some guys will blame it on their baldness or weight or even employment status. We usually don't even think that it could just be a matter of interpersonal connection (or lack thereof).

Talk in terms of the relationship. In cases where the guy is a friend, I understand that a woman really *does* appreciate the guy and doesn't want him to feel like a heel. She's probably also confused right now about my rule not to flatter him. The key is to keep language rooted in what's right for the relationship and not about the individual.

A co-worker of mine said: "Women should probably say, 'I think our relationship is best as a friendship.' Guys need to understand that the rejection isn't about what one person or the other wants but about the interpersonal dynamic—it's magic and mutual, or it isn't."

Affirm the friendship. In keeping the answer centered on the relationship and interaction, affirm the friendship. You can even let us know you're flattered we'd think of you that way. But just let us know that you don't want us to disappear forever. I asked out a casual acquaintance once who said, "I hope this doesn't mean you'll quit talking with me about music!" That helped me know she didn't think our relationship was calling for dating, but she appreciated our interaction.

One warning: affirming the relationship doesn't end with one conversation. "The denial is bad, but the time after the denial can be more painful," my friend Jim said. "While a message is sent with a denial, much larger messages can be sent in the weeks/ months following the rejection depending on how women handle the relationship."

That girl who asked me if I'd still talk music with her never IMed, emailed, or called me again. So to me, her actions overwrote anything she'd said. I felt it was her move to establish normalcy again, and it never happened. It's very hard for guys to know how to handle contact with a girl after rejection. We don't want to come on too strong. We don't want to make things weirder. So, while a woman doesn't want to send mixed messages, I believe the ball is in her court to give us a small sign that she wants the friendship. Not only does this help individual relationships, but maybe it takes a small step at bridging the gap of bitterness between men and women.

THE GALLERY OF LOST LOVES

Camerin: Sometimes post-breakup we do skew toward bitterness; other times we just feel overwhelming pain—pledging never to love, date, trust, or even look at a member of the opposite gender ever again. Some people use this as an excuse and an explanation as to why they've "kissed dating good-bye." But despite the pain we all feel after the final good-bye (even the pain I myself have felt over the years), I still argue that there's good to be found in the process between "well, hello there" and "have a nice life."

I came to this conclusion shortly after experiencing another striking a-ha realization: while all of the guys I've dated over the years have held a place in my heart, three of them have also held another piece of prize real estate—a spot on the wall above my couch or my bed. You see, these guys have either given me, helped me pick out, or assisted me in hanging the few pieces of "nice artwork" I own.

The first was from Mark, my first post-college boyfriend. He bought me a cool photograph of a lovely tree-lined trail in Central Park. When we broke up after three years of off-and-on dating, looking at this poster made me ache. But I still couldn't bring myself to take it down. Doing so would leave completely bare walls and seemingly another hole in my existence. So it remained . . . and eventually stopped being a Symbolic Reminder and finally became just a nice picture of a park.

Then there was the vintage Paris poster that Chris helped me pick out on our very first outing. A week later, he went with me to pick out matting and a frame. Seeing that poster on my bedroom wall reminded me of the first days of our dating. One day, long after we were "over," I was finally able to look at it with appreciation for the memories and joke to myself, "We'll always have Paris."

My most recent love interest helped me hang the picture currently over my couch. I admit I was nervous at first when he stood precariously on my couch with my power drill in his hands and tried valiantly to figure out how to put a nail hole in my apartment's finicky plaster wall without turning the entire thing to fine white powder. But there was something so endearing about having someone climb on my furniture and try to conquer my decorating dilemma for me, I was more than willing to take a risk and let him have a go at it.

It's not as though I ever set out to make artwork my "thing" with the guys I date. Just in the natural progression of spending time together we've shared these objects, these moments. In the days and weeks right after the guy is gone, it's been easy to question why I allow something so visible and key to my home environment to be affected by these entanglements of the heart. Sometimes it's easy to wonder why I even allow myself to open up to another shot at lasting love when it seems like another exercise in disappointment or pain. Why date? Why trust? Why risk the pain of good-bye I've experienced in every romantic relationship I've ever been in?

I remember sitting on my couch after my most recent breakup, looking at the picture he helped me hang, feeling the familiar sad ache, and thinking I should have learned better by now than to continually find myself living in a gallery of past relationships.

But then I took a good look at the rest of my walls and decorated spaces. There's a clock from Lisa, a cool candle holder from Jen, a poster from my sister and brother-in-law, a three-foot-high Eiffel Tower from Kathryn. My friends and family are all around me with these things. This isn't just a showcase of past loves, it's a gallery of all the people who've made an impact on my life.

I'm beginning to realize that in some ways, I'm a gallery of all these people too—with impressions of each of these people hanging somewhere in my being, making up the whole of this gallery showing, making me who I am. The friends have made me happy and more Christlike. The family members have made me secure and brave. Even the lost loves have made me stronger and wiser and richer. It was one of these loved ones who reminded me recently that God doesn't waste anything. The God who redeems can take even the most painful experience in my life and mold something beautiful from it. It's one of my favorite of his specialties—creating beauty from ashes (Isa. 61:3). And when I remember that each of these "people portraits" in my life is God's workmanship (Eph. 2:10), I realize they're all treasured and needed and beautiful.

And because of that, I'll continue to keep some wall space open . . . in my home, in my heart, in my life.

I now realize that every love and loss, every person and relationship, every broken heart and glimmer of hope that comes from dating as a grown-up goes into creating the messy work in progress that is me.

PARTING **THOUGHTS**

TODD and *Camerin:* As you navigate your own singleness journey—beginnings to breakups—we pray these thoughts and insights serve as a road sign pointing you in a positive and godly direction. Bon voyage!

Acknowledgments

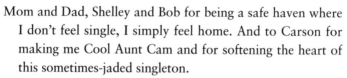

Camerin thanks:

Mom and Dad, Shelley and Bob for being a safe haven where I don't feel single, I simply feel home. And to Carson for making me Cool Aunt Cam and for softening the heart of this sometimes-jaded singleton.

The readers of my singles column at ChristianSinglesToday .com. I never tire of reading your empathetic, encouraging, kooky, heartbreaking, angry, and elated emails. Sharing this single journey with you is a privilege.

Todd for saying yes to this crazy project. I couldn't have done this book justice without your testosterone-tinged perspective. And it wouldn't have been near as much fun.

And the brilliant soul who created the Raspberry Lite White Berry at Caribou Coffee. I couldn't have done this without you.

TODD thanks:

My parents, for sacrificing for me and pushing me so I could have opportunities you didn't, Chad and Michelle for letting me be "the good son," and my entire family for supporting me even when my plans and dreams seem crazy.

The Hinsdale United Methodist Church youth group and leaders, for giving me a family away from home, for letting me slip away for so long to write this, and for every time you all asked how it was going.

Camerin, for coming up with this ridiculous idea, letting me ride your coattails, helping me believe I could do this thing, and of course, your friendship.

And the woman who played Becca on *Life Goes On* for being among the first to help me realize girls are pretty cool.

 **Camerin** and **TODD** thank:

Our friends for listening to us gripe, supporting us, and teaching us much of what we know about relationships. To our respective ex-boyfriends and ex-girlfriends for sharing part of the journey and for enriching our lives. To everyone who shared their dating (or lack thereof) stories with us.

Our homie LaTonya for being there, for putting up with all our "book talk," and for the spontaneous coffee and dinner runs that helped us stay sane.

Our personal photographer/favorite rock star Max for the glamour shots, blog props, and friendship.

The people at Christianity Today International who nurtured and invested in us as writers and editors. And to the company itself for graciously letting us reprint some of this material—and, of course, for the paychecks.

And, most importantly, God for using all our relationship confusion, hardships, and even brokenness in a way we could've never imagined. This has nothing to do with us, and all to do with you.

Notes

1. Rob Marus, "Kissing Nonsense Goodbye," *Christianity Today*, June 11, 2001, 46.

2. Ibid.

3. Barbara Dafoe Whitehead and David Popenoe, "The State of Our Union 2002," the National Marriage Project, June 2002, 21.

4. "The State of the Church, 2000," the Barna Group, Ltd., March 21, 2000.

5. John Eldredge, *Wild at Heart* (Nashville: Thomas Nelson, 2001), 6–7.

6. Walter Wangerin Jr., *As for Me and My House* (Nashville: Thomas Nelson, 1990), 142.

7. Larry Jackson, "Becoming the Spiritual Leader of Your Home," Promise Keepers newsletter, article reprinted online with permission, www.beliefnet. com/story/16/story_1627_1.html.

8. Wangerin, *As for Me and My House*, 149.

9. Henry Cloud, *How to Get a Date Worth Keeping* (Grand Rapids: Zondervan, 2005), 231–32.

10. Zen Lee, "When Dating Becomes a Mission," *Columbia Standard*, March 1997.

11. Terry Mattingly, "Missionary Cohabitating," Scripps Howard News Service, 2000.

12. Lauren F. Winner, *Real Sex* (Grand Rapids: Brazos, 2005), 15.

13. Song lyrics to "Deathtrap Daisy" (©2004 by Flicker USA Publishing, from the Flicker Records release *Staple* by Staple) are used by permission.

14. Beth Forbes, "Firm Believers More Likely to Be Flabby, Purdue Study Finds," *Purdue News*, March 1998.

15. Randolph E. Schmid, "Married People Healthier than Singles, Divorced, Others," Associated Press, Dec. 15, 2004.

16. Mike Powers, "In the Eye of the Beholder," *Human Ecology Forum*, Cornell University, Fall 1996, 16.

17. Ibid., 18.

18. Thomas Merton, *Thoughts in Solitude* (New York: Farrar, Straus and Giroux, 1958), 79.

19. Jennifer Croly, *Missing Being Mrs.* (Grand Rapids: Kregel, 2004), 152.

Camerin Courtney is editor of *Today's Christian Woman* and is the author of *Table for One*. She lives in Glen Ellyn, Illinois.

Todd Hertz is an editor for *Campus Life* magazine and *Christianity Today* online. He lives in Glendale Heights, Illinois.

88
489
× 39 months
4401
1467

$19,071